Praise for
Jerome Charyn

"Jerome Charyn is one of the most important writers in American literature." —**Michael Chabon**

"One of our finest writers. . . . Whatever milieu [Charyn] chooses to inhabit . . . his sentences are pure vernacular music, his voice unmistakable." —**Jonathan Lethem**

"Charyn, like Nabokov, is that most fiendish sort of writer— so seductive as to beg imitation, so singular as to make imitation impossible." —**Tom Bissell**

"Among Charyn's writerly gifts is a dazzling energy. . . . [He is] an exuberant chronicler of the mythos of American life." —**Joyce Carol Oates,** *New York Review of Books*

"Charyn skillfully breathes life into historical icons." —*New Yorker*

"Both a serious writer and an immensely approachable one, always witty and readable." —*Washington Post*

"Absolutely unique among American writers." —*Los Angeles Times*

"A contemporary American Balzac." —*Newsday*

IN THE
SHADOW
OF
KING SAUL

Also by
Jerome Charyn
(most recent titles)

———————————

Johnny One-Eye: A Tale of the American Revolution
(2008)

The Secret Life of Emily Dickinson (2010)

Joe DiMaggio: The Long Vigil (2011)

I Am Abraham: A Novel of Lincoln and the Civil War
(2014)

Bitter Bronx: Thirteen Stories (2015)

A Loaded Gun: Emily Dickinson for the 21st Century
(2016)

Jerzy: A Novel (2017)

IN THE
SHADOW
OF
KING SAUL

ESSAYS ON SILENCE AND SONG

Jerome Charyn

THE ART OF THE ESSAY

BELLEVUE LITERARY PRESS
New York

THE ART OF THE ESSAY SERIES

Bellevue Literary Press's The Art of the Essay series features compelling,
creative nonfiction from accomplished writers of fiction,
demonstrating the Bellevue Literary Press belief that fine literature
knows no boundaries of genre or imagination.

ALSO IN THIS SERIES:
A Solemn Pleasure by Melissa Pritchard

First published in the United States in 2018 by Bellevue Literary Press, New York

For information, contact:
Bellevue Literary Press
www.blpress.org

Library of Congress Cataloging-in-Publication Data

Names: Charyn, Jerome, author.
Title: In the shadow of King Saul : essays on silence and song / Jerome Charyn.
Description: First edition. | New York : Bellevue Literary Press, 2018. | Series: The art
of the essay ; 2 | Includes bibliographical references. |
Identifiers: LCCN 2017039517 (print) | LCCN 2018028253 (ebook) |
ISBN 9781942658436 (e-book) | ISBN 9781942658429 (pbk.) |
ISBN 9781942658436 (ebook)
Subjects: LCSH: Charyn, Jerome—Childhood and youth. | Charyn, Jerome—Homes
and haunts. | Novelists, American—20th century—Biography. | Children of
immigrants—New York (State)—New York. | Bronx (New York, N.Y.)—Social
life and customs.
Classification: LCC PS3553.H33 (ebook) | LCC PS3553.H33 Z46 2018 (print) |
DDC 814/.54 [B] —dc23
LC record available at https://lccn.loc.gov/2017039517

 This publication is made possible by the New York
State Council on the Arts with the support of Governor
Andrew M. Cuomo and the New York State Legislature.

 This project is supported in part
by an award from the National
Endowment for the Arts.

Bellevue Literary Press would like to thank all its generous
donors—individuals and foundations—for their support.

Book design and composition by Mulberry Tree Press, Inc.

Manufactured in the United States of America.

First Edition

1 3 5 7 9 8 6 4 2

paperback ISBN: 978-1-942658-42-9
ebook ISBN: 978-1-942658-43-6

In memory of

"Makhno," Nathalie Babel

(1929–2005)

CONTENTS

Silence & Song

1

I WAS ALWAYS A LITTLE SADDENED BY SAUL, the Bible's very first king, who did not have the gift of song. Saul lived in a silent universe. He was tone-deaf. Nothing he did could ever please the Lord. Young David had his lyre and his slingshot; David was the anointed one. He killed Goliath with a single stone, while Saul's last act of grace was to fall upon his own sword. Saul was among the living dead, even while he served as king. The Lord would not look upon him and was deaf to his silent songs.

Stripped of his royal robes, Saul could have come from the South Bronx, which was also a region of silence. It was a blighted, barren landscape. There were no libraries or bookshops in my corner of the Bronx, only stationery stores with dime detective novels and Classic Comics— the tattered rags of culture we had left. I learned to read from comic books, where words loomed like quicksilver as they shifted from panel to panel and then disappeared. These were illustrated classics, of course. So we

had Ivanhoe and that villainous Knight Templar Brian de
Bois-Guilbert, who lusted after Jewish maidens; Michael
Strogoff and the white wolves he wrestled with in the
taiga; Natty Bumppo with his deer rifle that was as long
as a lance. Even then, at eight, I knew that something was
amiss in these tales. The art never varied, did not have its
own signature or song. It was static, as if created out of
a cookie cutter. The Deerslayer and all the other characters in the pantheon of Classic Comics had the identical
carapace of ink and color. I had to rely on another cultural
rag—the movie house—if I wanted a bit of romance.

Call it the Dover, the Zenith, the Luxor, the Earl,
or the Ritz. They were all shoe boxes sandwiched into
a vacant lot, cellars above ground, where a boy could
spend a Saturday afternoon in the dark, attached by
some invisible thread to ghosts on the wall who were
much more vital than my own phantomatic self. I
could have been born in any of these shoe boxes rather
than at Bronx County Hospital . . .

I wrote to Alan Ladd, c/o Paramount, and received
a snapshot in the mail with his personal signature. It was
near the end of World War II, and the studio must have
sat him down once or twice a week and had him scratch
his name several thousand times, in lieu of military service. I'd seen him in *The Glass Key* and *This Gun for Hire*,
both released in 1942, but such black-and-white classics
didn't arrive at the Dover until 1944. He had sad eyes and
seldom talked in *This Gun for Hire*. His sentences merely
punctuated his long silences. He had a partner on the

screen, Veronica Lake, who wore a lock of blond hair over one eye. She was either silent or sang out a sentence or two. I followed their film careers. Ladd went on to play a gunslinger who's forced out of retirement in *Shane* (1953). It was his pivotal role—sad-eyed as ever, his only bark was with his gun. Meanwhile, Veronica Lake fell into oblivion after a bout with the bottle. Living under an assumed name, she ended up as a waitress at the Martha Washington, a women's boardinghouse-hotel in Manhattan, and died of cirrhosis of the liver at the age of fifty. Ladd also died at fifty, after gulping a lethal cocktail of alcohol and barbiturates. But these ghosts on the wall—and others like them—really mattered to a wild child like me. All my language and lust would come from the movies.

Public school was a waste of time. I was hopeless at spelling bees. I couldn't master long division. The sachems at the Board of Education decided that the underprivileged dwarfs of the South Bronx should play a musical instrument. And they settled on one called the ocarina, a poor boy and girl's hybrid harmonica and flute, made of pure plastic. I never learned to play a note. My piping on the ocarina was flat and dry, without a gob of spit. Whatever education I had, musical or not, was picked up on the sly at the Zenith or the Earl. That's where I taught myself to rhumba, while I watched Rita Hayworth tantalize a whole cadre of men in *Gilda* (1946).

I had little need of a notebook or lead pencil in the dark. I imitated whatever I saw on the screen with some primitive pantomime inside my skull. I discovered that people actually talked at dinnertime, as I watched Irene Dunne hold several conversations while she gathered peas with a knife and fork. At home, we grabbed with our hands and gobbled our food in silence. I can't say if it was part of some Talmudic law handed down to my parents, both of whom were born inside the Pale of Settlement decreed by the czar and his clever band of plunderers and scribes. Was silence during meals considered some sacred ritual, both a blessing and a curse? I'm not sure. We never spoke—not about politics, or Bronx culture, or my daily misdeeds. My father did grunt and groan. My very existence seemed to bother him. He could not bear to look at me. Was it out of some primordial jealousy? He was abandoned as a boy, left within the Pale, because he had conjunctivitis—pinkeye—and couldn't travel to the New World with his mother, brother, and sister in the bowels of an ocean liner sailing out of Bremen. He was presented with a violin to console him. And that is the most treasured photo I have of my father—with his fiddle. He must have scratched plenty of sad tunes on its strings. His pinkeye cleared up after seventeen months and he sailed out of Bremen before his sixteenth birthday. All families must have been toxic to him after that—soon as I got up from the table, he would call me in his Polish jargon a "house wolf" who fattened myself on my own father's flesh. It was the insane idea of someone who'd been left to fiddle all alone.

Perhaps I was a house wolf, but I still wasn't clever enough to realize that he suffered from a lifelong depression. Besides, he was desperately in love with my mother, Faigele, a dark-eyed Aphrodite who had an uncanny resemblance to Joan Crawford, Merle Oberon, and Gene Tierney, depending on the sunlight and the time of day. I'm pretty certain she didn't love him back. I had become her confidant long before I started kindergarten. And the Zenith soon made me precocious about the arcane rituals of love.

Faigele would mimic her own disgust at the very thought of my father touching her. Why, oh why, did my mother ever marry him? It wasn't a simple tale. Faigele's own mother had died when she was two. Her father had already gone to America to seek his fortune. And when my mother arrived fifteen years later, she had to deal with a stepmother and her father's second family. "Faigele," which means little bird in Yiddish, didn't have much of a nest in the New World. She went to night school on Manhattan's Lower East Side, where she met Samuel Charyn, a young machine operator in a fur factory, who could cut mink collars with all the art of Michelangelo, despite the forlorn, half-crazed look in his eye. He followed Faigele home from night school. "A furrier is like a doctor," Faigele's stepmother whispered like a poison pellet in her ear—it served as a brutal shove out the door. My mother and father were married and moved to the South Bronx, where my older brother, Harvey, was born in 1934. He was "a colic baby," who cried all the time, my mother told me. Perhaps my father read his old abandonment and bitter fate in my brother's cries. Harve was no rival. And then I was born three years later. I never cried once from the moment I left the womb, according to my mother's testimony. I must have seemed like a sinister cherub to Sam, put there as a permanent travail, to test my mother's devotion to him. I do not remember being pampered. I slept in a crib. I fed myself like an infant prodigy, while my mother had to stuff food into Harvey's mouth until he was eight. What I do remember are my father's rumblings, and that look of rage.

My brother had rickets and had to sit in the sun, but rickets couldn't hobble him. He loped about his domain. He was fearless from the age of five. He could be cruel, like any battler and young king of the block, but he seldom allied himself with my father against me. I was Harve's kid brother, and that bestowed a certain bounty on me that was almost like an invisible letter of transit. I could trot into any neighborhood and was never hassled. "Hey," some local chieftain would announce to his vassals, "that's Charyn's kid brother. Leave him alone."

Harve never backed away from a fight. He would become a bodybuilder and enter the Mr. New York City contest at the age of fifteen. It was in the golden age of bodybuilding—the 1950s—when every sand dune had its own contingent of barbells and mats for somersaults and handstands. The mecca of all bodybuilders was the south side of Santa Monica Pier, with its mythic Muscle Beach, the home and training ground of past, present, and future Mr. Americas. As a kid, I didn't quite understand the erotic charge of men gazing at other men, or the mystery of male photographers who ran after Harve. I dreamt of becoming Mr. America, like John Grimek, George Eiferman, and Clarence Ross (mostly unremembered now); Grimek had one glass eye and a godlike physique. I didn't have his classic lines or his lineaments. My biceps were more like sweet peas than ostrich eggs.

Harve placed third, I think, at the Mr. New York City pageant, and won the consolation prize of Most Muscular Man. He abandoned bodybuilding after that, and so did I, but I couldn't have preserved my sanity without his presence. My father had remained a stunted child, lost in imaginary ailments, suffering from an ulcer that never revealed itself in any barium X-ray. I remember sitting with him on the Seventh Avenue Local when I was nine, because he worried that he might faint on the ride to a prominent stomach specialist and didn't want to die all alone in a subway car. It was the first time I'd entered the maze of Manhattan. We had to board the Forty-second Street Shuttle, a curious train that seemed to arrive out of nowhere and stop on a platform that had retracting metal claws. This shuttle brought us into the bowels of Grand Central Station. My father and I had to walk half a mile to leave that underground labyrinth.

The specialist, who had an office near the Chrysler Building, and looked like a savant, with bushy eyebrows and dandruff on his white gown, could not find the least trace of an ulcer. To celebrate, my father purchased a car—a green Plymouth— right after the war and never learned to drive. He was in mortal terror as he sat behind the wheel, with me, his little hostage, in the backseat, watching him shiver as he approached the George Washington Bridge. A friend from the fur market served as his instructor.

"Sam, Sam, it's not a gondola. You have to stick to one lane."

Fear—and rage—defined him. He would lock me in the closet for no reason, slap me, or spit in my face if I refused to listen to one of his irrational demands. And even though I dreamt, Hamlet-like, of his destruction, with the fantasy of a house wolf growing large enough, and fat enough, to swallow him alive, the murder within my bones was mingled with pity. I must have internalized his pain and his silent song.

I went to Manhattan's High School of Music and Art, where I wore muscle T-shirts, and quickly grasped that my chiseled pectorals and tough-guy looks would get me nowhere with the luscious middle-class maidens of Central Park West. I got rid of my chartreuse saddle-stitch trousers, a Bronx staple, and wore white bucks and khakis, like all the Manhattan swains. I was an art student who painted in bold colors—the Gauguin of Boston Road—but didn't have the rudest gifts of a draftsman. I couldn't draw a cow or a human thumb with my piece of charcoal. The images wouldn't flow out of my head. I wanted to paint with words. Yet I had little language other than what I had appropriated from the Classic Comics. Other students at M & A read J. D. Salinger with a religious zeal and could talk of Tolstoy and Herman Hesse. They were also moviegoers. But I was lost around them, since Ingmar Bergman and Roberto Rossellini never got to the Ritz.

I went to a fancy barber. Wore a crew cut and looked like an Apache on the run. I didn't have my classmates' glibness, their gift of gab. They had talked at the dinner table all their lives, while I hungered for words. The movies had made me into an excellent mime. I memorized the musical rhythms and speech patterns of Riverside Drive and Central Park West. I felt like a spy among modern Knights Templar, a burglar breaking into an exclusive clan. I tried to write. But all I had was cunning and a reclusive silence. I didn't even have a reading list except for what I could burgle from class discussions.

I took a creative writing class with the chairman of the English Department, a Scotsman named Dr. McCloud. He asked us all to hand something in—a page, a paragraph, a line of poetry or prose—every class. I scribbled the diary of a house wolf, with all its limits and lamentations. I couldn't summon up a lexicon I didn't have. All I could offer were my Bronx horizons. While Ramona S., the class poet and future valedictorian, discussed the prominent artists and writers who had visited her mother's Central Park West salon, I described the feral cats in the backyard of my Bronx tenement. I had spent hours observing these cats and their routines, how they had their own royal retinue, a king and queen with battle scars. But I couldn't compete with the artists and writers in Ramona's galaxy. I wasn't a conjurer or a poet. I had no silky words hidden in my sleeve. The other students didn't have my monklike devotion to the page. A senior class in creative writing couldn't affect the barometric rise and fall of their College Boards. They had Yale and Vassar to think about. But Ramona basked in the glory of her ocher-colored report card. Dr. McCloud had given her the grade of 99—a pinch short of perfection. I was startled when I sneaked a glance at my own card. Some clerk must have made a grievous error. My final grade in McCloud's class was a flat 100. I ran to his office like a little thief.

"Sir, Ramona has much more finesse. I had to scratch and scratch for every word."

He smiled behind his Scottish mustache. "Yes, and she hardly scratched at all."

2

I whistled my way into Columbia College without racking up supersonic scores on my College Boards. Perhaps I was admitted from within the Pale of the South Bronx through some extraordinary quota—a provision for the poorest Jews on the planet. My father hadn't worked in years. There was turmoil in the fur market. It was during the McCarthy witch hunts. Communists had been discovered within the ranks of my father's union, and the Justice Department had to weed them out. This was a slow process. Besides, my father's imaginary illnesses had multiplied. He barely left the house for weeks at a time.

Meanwhile, I was discovering a wonderland of books—it was like plunging deeper and deeper into a rabbit hole.

I remember teachers and students whispering about an arcane writer in a bowler hat, with big ears, Franz Kafka, who worked at an insurance company in Prague and scribbled novels and tales at night about a hunger artist, or a beetle with a beetle's legs and a human brain, or his own mysterious double, Josef K., who went from one bureaucratic nightmare to the next, looking for the least sign of sanity. Reading Kafka was charged with erotic bewilderment, like some primal scream of love.

I began to build my own castle of Modern Library classics, with one bookcase piled upon another. I fingered every book with a rabbinical devotion, scanned every word, groped about with a blind king called Oedipus, shared Philoctetes' festering wound and his magic bow, became an ax murderer like Raskolnikov, struggled against the Lilliputians with Gulliver, until I had my own plastic presence, could shift from shape to shape, gender to gender. Anna Karenina one moment, Gregor Samsa the next. There was a holiness to the written word, and a danger. It was filled with a fire that could sear your guts and scar your soul. There was no other route than surrendering to this danger zone. I imagined a lifelong apprenticeship, as I learned and relearned my craft. I would become a poor man's Spinoza, a polisher of words. I sought ways and means to support my apprenticeship.

I decided to become an intelligence officer in the air force. I imagined that I would sit at some secret air base for twenty years and study the path of Russian stealth bombers, while I wrote at night. I had Kafka's big ears. What else did I need? I could collect my pension and continue my apprenticeship, retire to some secluded village in the south of France and live off my monthly allotment of dollars.

I was sent to an air base on Long Island. I had to spend the night, and I was given a room in the officers' dorm. I remember the narrow bed and the tiny bureau—it was like a monk's cell. I met with a little jury of captains and colonels. It felt like an inquisition. I wanted to catch Russian spies and spy planes. I assumed these savants would evaluate my rudimentary knowledge of tradecraft, like a bunch of chess wizards. I would match my skills with theirs. Pawn to king 4 . . .

These savants weren't interested in tradecraft, or any craft at all. They concerned themselves with my ardor for the military. I was asked to name the current Secretary of Defense and Chairman of the Joint Chiefs of Staff. I didn't have a clue.

I had to seek another source of income.

I entered a Teacher Ed program at Hunter College and became a substitute in the city's high schools. Success or failure depended upon a particular knack. I registered with one school, my alma mater, Music and Art. Hence, I was always available, and the school clerk would call me first when another English teacher was ill. It was a much better plan than looking for stealth bombers. I taught once or twice a week and earned enough to survive. My home was a closet in Washington Heights, with a hot plate, a fridge, a toilet, and a desk that faced a brick wall. I didn't feel deprived in the least, but how would I learn my tradecraft? I read Nabokov and James Joyce, and shuddered at the musicality of their lines. *Lolita* was like one endless song, and all I had were memories of my ocarina. I did not possess a magic flute. I would never have the absolute pitch of that half-blind Irish wayfarer, or Nabokov's ability to bend and twist my own native tongue. Nor was I an adventurer, like Isaac Babel, who rode with the Red Cavalry, and scribbled tales about Jewish gangsters in Odessa. Benya Krik's orange pantaloons were as sensuous as musical notes. Nothing can stab the human heart like a period put in the right place, Babel wrote in a story about his own escapades as a young Jewish writer living in Petersburg without a residence permit. And all I had was the Bronx . . .

3

I FILLED THAT DESOLATE VOID with my imagination. There were plenty of gangsters in the South Bronx, though none with Benya's orange pants or his eloquence. Silence reigned here, the silence of Saul. My brother Harvey had become a homicide detective in the wilds of Brooklyn. I remember his personal Calvary in order to be a cop. He was ¼ of an inch too short, and he had to stretch for hours at a time against a board to reach the requisite height of five-eight. He'd also had a few run-ins with the law—a *near* arrest, speeding tickets, stuff like that. He was given an investigator, who carried a file with esoteric scribbles on its dun-colored jacket that could have come straight out of Kafka. I met this investigator, who had gray hair and wore gray—gray socks, gray tie—and had a gray complexion. He poked around, tried to get me to squeal on my own brother.

"Come on, kid. Was Harve involved in any local robberies?"

"He didn't have the time," I said. "He was building up his biceps and studying to be an exemplary cop."

This gray man curled his eyebrows with curiosity. "And what did he study?"

"How to protect old people and blind people in the South Bronx," I said, with all the panache of my favorite delinquent, Huckleberry Finn. Harve got through the investigation and was shipped off to the Police Academy, where he graduated with a trophy as the best marksman in his class. He was a motorcycle cop for a while, and was now with Brooklyn Homicide. He had the same sadness in his eyes that he'd had as a child. He didn't have my rabbinical lust for words. As a Jewish cop in a land of Irishers, he was the first to break through the door during an arrest. He carried a shotgun in a shopping bag. Meanwhile, I searched and searched for my own song, a melody that would have my imprint, and mine alone. I didn't believe in metaphysics—meaning, for me, existed in the invisible web between silence and song. Benya Krik had his orange pants, but his long silences as Odessa's king of crime were often far more persuasive than the shots he fired in the air to frighten fellow gangsters. There was also violence in his movements and in his verbs. Language, I had always believed, was a violent activity. The first scratch on a page was a kind of violation, breaking through a void of white. And then the music begins, that internal, twisting rhyme of word upon word.

What is Huck Finn's tale other than a song of isolation and sadness, of growing up in a world of untruths? Huck's truths are the lies he tells, to protect a runaway slave and keep up his own moral courage against a host of swindlers, connivers, and thieves. He has to *steal* language, like bolts of thunder, in order to survive.

But thunderbolts are hard to find. I wrote a story about an idiot girl, called her Faigele, as a coded message to my mother. This *idiotke* had one ambition—she wanted to fly. I imposed myself upon her tale, became her narrator, a young scrivener who leaves home and serves his apprenticeship on the Lower East Side, where Faigele haunts the rooftops and tumbles to her death when her flapping arms fail her as necessary wings. But in my own psyche, her need to fly was akin to the writer's art—the desire to overreach, to move beyond the limits of language itself.

The story was published, and I became a local celebrity for a month or so. "Faigele the Idiotke" was noticed by the principal of Music and Art. I'd been teaching there, steadily, religiously, for two years, like a samurai warrior on long stints. If a tenured English teacher suffered a heart attack, I was called in and might teach in his stead for months at a time. It was ideal, almost. I could sit in the faculty lunchroom with former teachers of mine. Few other graduates had ever come back to teach. I could create my own syllabus, talk about the *politics* of art—how language could wound or heal, often in the same wind of words.

I loved the students, and I suspect they loved me. I was a dynamiter, unlike the career teachers they had. I was there to shake them up, rouse them, to shift their sensibilities and points of view. But I had a bit of a problem. I couldn't work on a novel while I was part of the full-time faculty. I had to grade 150 compositions every other week, rewrite entire paragraphs, like some magical scribe. I was relieved when the teacher whose slot I was filling recovered from his heart attack. I could then return to my old stint as a samurai and get back to writing. But the damage had already been done.

The principal called me into his office. He was the only member of the administration who had his own private toilet, like a little king on a porcelain throne. He had a copy of "Faigele" on his desk.

"Where does it all come from?" he asked. "How did you manage to make up a girl with imaginary wings?"

The wings were real, I wanted to say. They just happened to fail her. But I didn't want to be a smart aleck. "I guess I have a hyperbolic imagination," I said.

His eyes shone with the clarity of a prince.

"That's my whole point," he said, slapping his desk with a tiny fist that looked like a bird's skull. "It's exactly what we need at this school. I'm willing to make an exception and open up a line."

He was a bit surly at my silence. This principal with his own toilet had to repeat himself. "Didn't you hear me? Open up a line."

I was still confused.

"You're a sub," he said. "You have no claims on us. You haven't been offered a permanent contract. And I'm opening up a line to put you on a tenure track. Shall I tell you how many teachers have applied for a position at M & A?"

He dug into his top drawer and pulled out a file as fat as a dictionary, stuffed with letters that had begun to ripen with age. "I don't even bother to read them anymore. I could run a Lonely Hearts club with what they write. There are no jobs, and I'm offering you one."

"Why?" I asked, with my own quirky defiance. It was his porcelain throne that bothered me, his sense of privilege. No, it wasn't that. I was frightened to death of his offer. I would have devoted myself to these kids, proved to them that Hamlet was a psychopath, a killer who believed in ghosts, and that Richard III was a hunchback who climbed his way to a kingdom on nothing else than a rickety ladder of words. And "Mr. C.," as I was known at this castle on a hill, after thirty years of tenure at Music and Art behind him, would have remained bone-dry, a writer who couldn't write.

"*Why?* It's impertinent to ask such a question. We

want you, and I'm willing to rip up all the other letters and create a line."

His face turned dark and bitter when I refused him.

"Think," he said, like a man issuing a summons.

I still said no.

"Think again."

He left me there and went into his private throne. He could have scratched me off the substitute list. But I was still the samurai, first to be called. He was even gallant whenever we met in the halls, with a slightly mocking tone.

"Our Mr. C.," he said.

I returned to my closet in Washington Heights. It had once been an examining room attached to a doctor's office on the ground floor at 333 Fort Washington Avenue, across from a playground and a little park that led to the George Washington Bridge. I was burgled after I'd been at this address for a year. The burglar broke in by climbing over a gate with metal spears in the backyard. He must have been desperate. I had nothing but rags and a notebook. He took all the clothes out of my armoire, except for one corduroy jacket, as if he were leaving me my last bit of panoply as a samurai.

The doctor, who was about eighty years old and also my landlord, had iron bars installed outside my window to protect me from other intruders. And that's how I lived, on cans of tuna fish. I didn't have one painting on the wall, not even a mirror. But I felt privileged, without a single encumbrance.

Friends of mine from college got married, finished graduate school, became scholars or students at the Iowa Writers' Workshop. They studied with Philip Roth, or another mentor, who whisked them off to Manhattan publishing houses like paper airplanes, while I had to settle in with a novice dentist at the Columbia Dental College, a first-year student in the teeth of his own apprenticeship. I was sort of a charity case with a blue card that said I didn't earn enough to pay for the care of my gums. The dental college was on the eighth floor of Vanderbilt Clinic, a few blocks from where I lived. I occupied a dental chair among an endless maze of chairs. The novices wore blue gowns and were supervised by their own savants. My novice was from Newark. His name was Phil. And he was on a mission that wasn't so removed from mine. He wanted to master the art of dentistry and remain at the college until he was a dental wizard. His father was also a dentist and paid a fortune to keep Phil at the clinic, but Phil had no desire to join his father's practice, or any practice at all.

"Most dentists are crooks," he claimed.

"What about your dad?" I mumbled, with one of Phil's instruments in my mouth, ripping away at all the plaque.

"The biggest crook of all—pulls teeth that don't have to be pulled, charges a king's ransom for mundane root-canal work."

"Phil, he's your father."

"He's still a crook."

Phil's grand scheme was to remain at the clinic and hold on to this chair for as long as he could. It was curious, because his teeth were quite yellow. But I had faith in Phil, despite his megalomania—he wanted to be the most prodigious dental student on the planet, with his point of service limited to one chair. It was no more insane than my own desires. I struggled at my craft. I wondered if words themselves induced madness, if the tundra and the turbulence inside Hamlet's head shaped him into a destroyer of civilizations and social order. Left to his own devices, he would have killed, killed, killed, found other ghosts in a closet, stabbed through other curtains. He was no less bloody than the king's hired assassins, Rosencrantz and Guildenstern. And all his delusions were wrapped in a cloak of language.

I wasn't Hamlet. I wasn't even Huck Finn. I was a manchild in a rented room. And I was prepared to stay there for the rest of my life, lost in the belief that I could crack my own language code, create melodies from strings of sentences. Language itself was like a lance—or a hatchet, murderous with all its music.

I might have ended up at Bellevue. But "Faigele the Idiotke" had brought me seductive missives from half a dozen publishers. And I slipped into the role of a published novelist rather than a true pioneer. I had to give up my apprenticeship, my closet in Washington Heights, and my renegade dental student, and I rode across the continent to Palo Alto and Stanford University as a visiting professor. It was only the beginning of my wanderlust. I spent half a year in Barcelona's Gothic Quarter, eating black paella—made from the juicy ink of squid—and listening to the sound of medieval stones. The Gothic Quarter had its own mournful music. . . .

I lived in Houston for a while, rode the mechanical bull at Gilley's, survived a tempest that ripped out every other roof on my quiet street near Rice University, where I was still a samurai, teaching for a semester. I moved to Paris, sat next to Sartre at La Coupole, a landmark brasserie in Montparnasse; half-blind, he scribbled words as large as a child's building blocks with his golden pen. He was the *maître*, our Voltaire; La Coupole's staff spun around him while he worked in noble silence.

I visited Bonn and the house where Beethoven was born, his bed no larger than a crib. He must have slept all curled up, in a fetal position half his life. And that's how I saw myself, an enormous baby bursting through the roof of that dollhouse in Bonn. It did not matter where I went, or what I did. My psyche and the thump, thump inside my skull were still in that rented room on Fort Washington Avenue.

It's rather curious that I received an award from the Shomrim Society of Jewish policemen as Person of the Year, when all I ever wrote about were corrupt and crazy cops in my crime novels. But perhaps the Shomrim Society was far shrewder than I. I did, after all, sing the plangent song of most policemen, Jewish or not—none of them had the poetry to match the rough poetry of the streets. They were gunslingers, like Alan Ladd in *Shane*, but without the romantic chill of the Wild West. And so I'm left with the silence of my brother—he died of a damaged heart in 2015. And I roam the landscape without him, unable to mourn. I couldn't even commemorate him at his funeral; everyone, even family and friends, felt like a stranger. The love we shared was much too private. That's why I'm so drawn to Saul, the king who did not have a musical ear, who could not recite the simplest tune. A warrior abandoned by God, he did have a gift as great as David's lyre. Silence was his song.

THE PIECES COLLECTED HERE are my own lyrical autobiography. Several of the selections are about other writers, some celebrated, some forgotten—Saul Bellow, Anzia Yezierska, Samuel Ornitz, Herman Melville, Isaac Babel, and Louise Brooks, who happened to have also been a movie star once upon a time. All these writers scalped me in some way, left their mark.

Bellow was "a model and a manifest for a boy from the Bronx, a kind of open-sesame into the art of writing." He found his own rhythm, his own accent, in *The Adventures of Augie March* (1953). Its constant clatter is like living inside a hornet's head. There are no empty spaces in Bellow land; the book is an endless riff, a song about song itself. Augie March is a modern Huck Finn, marooned in a river of words. He invents himself on this river, with a mingling of Yiddish, the French argot of Quebec (where he lived as a young boy), gangster talk, the Torah, and Tolstoy. As Bellow lay dying, he slipped back into consciousness, looked up, and asked, "Was I a man or was I a jerk?" Somewhere within that sentence lies Bellow's great gift—his sense of wonder and entitlement about himself, coupled with a rattling insecurity.

Anzia Yezierska was never as famous as Bellow, but she did flourish for a while in the 1920s as a ghetto princess. She was born around 1880—the exact date is unclear. She arrived in America in 1901, according to critic Irving Howe, although it might have been much earlier. Who knows? She would never master the elasticity of the English language, yet there is a deep poignancy in her stuttering gait, that borrowed, twisted Yankee tongue of hers. And though she disappeared as a writer during her own lifetime (she died in a nursing home in 1970), she would be resurrected in the 1990s by a new generation of readers and writers. Yezierska had little sense of structure, as she herself admitted. "I can never learn to plot or plan. It's always a mystery how I even work out a beginning or an end of a story." She wrote like an amnesiac, with missing musical chords, trying desperately to exist "in the white spaces between the words." Her style of no style touches us somehow, and that *missing* lyricism, her stutter of words, continues to haunt us. Music, after all, and its absence, is an amazing witch.

Isaac Babel had all the elasticity that Yezierska lacked. Even in translation, his stories sing with a shattering intensity and rhythm. He was murdered by Stalin's henchmen in 1940, at the age of forty-five, shot in the back of the head. He could have emigrated permanently to France, but he felt that living without

the Russian language around him was a form of suicide. Stalin had a curious relationship with Babel, since
he loved Babel's writing, and spread rumors that Babel
was in some Siberian prison camp, so that the writer
remained a ghost for several years, with constant sight-
ings by some camp commandant. But the rich musicality of Babel's Odessa tales and the stark murmur of his
stories about the Red Cavalry survived Stalin's purges
and the crushing banality of the Soviet regime.

Babel was an underground man long before he
died. Addressing the Union of Soviet Writers in 1934, he
declared that he had become "the master of a new literary
genre, the genre of silence." Samuel Ornitz was another
underground man, whose whole life, like Babel's, was a
matter of silence and song. The son of a prosperous dry-
goods merchant, Ornitz chose to write about the mean
streets of Manhattan's Jewish ghetto. In 1923, Ornitz published a novel, *Haunch Paunch and Jowl*, disguised as "An
Anonymous Autobiography," written by a lower-court
judge. The novel is full of noise, like Bellow's *Augie March*,
but Ornitz's hero, Meyer Hirsch, is much more ambiguous, and lives at the rough edge between politics and
crime. The book was an enormous success. Still, Ornitz
never recaptured that magical stutter of the streets. Like
Anzia Yezierska, Ornitz went out to Hollywood. Yezierska fled as fast as she could, while Ornitz remained, and
worked on such screen classics as *King of the Newsboys* and
The Man Who Reclaimed His Head. He ended up in jail as
a member of the Hollywood Ten, who refused to testify

before the House Committee on Un-American Activities in 1947, and died of a stroke ten years later.

There's another Hollywood tale to tell, that of Louise Brooks. Born in Cherryvale, Kansas, in 1906, she was a movie star before she was twenty-one. There's never been another screen face as defiant and naughty as hers, as if she could cannibalize the movie-house wall. But it didn't last. Louise had a meteoric rise—and fall. She was forgotten by the time she was thirty. She moved to Rochester in 1956 without a dime. She lived like a nun and survived on strawberry jam. And she wrote short, prismatic essays about Hollywood that read like poetry in the cloth of prose. She captured the murderous siren's call of movieland. And she understood her own witchery on the screen. "The great art of films does not consist in descriptive movement of face and body, but in the movements of thought and soul transmitted in a kind of intense isolation." That isolation has a terrifying beauty.

And so we're back to silence and song. And I write about other silent heroes, such as Josh Gibson, the black Babe Ruth, who hid his rage behind a sweet, childlike disposition. He was voiceless without a baseball bat, fell into long silences. He couldn't define himself against the best white ballplayers, but had to barnstorm in the Negro Leagues, like a boy who could never grow up. He was obsessed with Joe DiMaggio, not with his money or his fame, but with his *visibility* as a baseball player in the big leagues. And as he turned inward and had violent outbursts, he was locked away in a mental ward, where he would sit alone in a chair by the window and have imaginary one-sided conversations with Joe DiMaggio.

"C'mon, Joe, talk to me, why don't you talk to me?"

He was allowed to leave the ward and play baseball on weekends. But soon he couldn't play at all; the voices in his head devoured him. He died in 1947, the same year Jackie Robinson broke into white baseball. Gibson was thirty-five.

He was one of my boyhood heroes.

Outliers and isolatoes such as Josh Gibson and Louise Brooks weave through the collection. A terrible sadness surrounds them, just as it surrounds King Saul. There's also Mayor Ed Koch, who could not live without his own tumult. He had an anger that was close to criminality, and also the playfulness of a delinquent. He once described New York City as his own personal grocery store. He could have been a character out of *Augie March*. He could also have been a king. Everyone feared him. I once watched him bully half a dozen real estate moguls, who cowered in his presence. He was a kind of golem, monstrous in his behavior, yet the mournful look he had almost redeemed him. His parents and mine passed through Ellis Island. That immigrant station is the centerpiece of my own story; it's where my imagination was cradled. I can see myself in the registry room, with inspectors considering every one of us as cattle. And there's my father, cured of pinkeye, clutching his violin. That fiddle is the music inside my head. And each scratch on its strings tells its own tale.

The Sadness of Saul
(1986)

(Author's note: The Revised Standard Version of the Bible is used in this essay.)

1

The first book of Samuel is about the presence and absence of voices, the history of a tribe that has become tone-deaf. The Hebrews have forgotten how to listen. They cannot hear God's voice. The Lord is absent from their lives. They go into battle with the Lord's own ark and lose it to the Philistines. It's a sad and evil time for the Hebrews. "And the word of the Lord was rare in those days; there was no frequent vision" (3:1).

Enter Samuel. He is God's chosen, the boy who was "lent to the Lord" (1:28). He grows into a prophet, priest, and judge of Israel. Samuel alone of all the Hebrews can hear God's voice. His nearness to God is the one bit of unity the Hebrews have. Samuel *is* the nation. But his own sons are bad priests, and the older Samuel gets, the more that "nation" begins to worry. The elders of Israel say to Samuel, "Behold, you are old and your sons do not walk in your ways; now appoint for us a king to govern us like all the nations" (8:4). Uneasy about the notion of a king, Samuel prays to the Lord, and the Lord tells him, "Hearken to the voice of the people in all that they say to you; for they have not rejected you, but they have rejected me from being king over them" (8:7).

And the child of that rejection is Saul. The Lord chooses him as Israel's first secular king. He's handsome and tall. "There is none like him among all the people" (10:24). But Saul hides among his family's baggage when Samuel comes to fetch him. He's an outcast from the moment he's anointed by Samuel. He's the very idea of king as a lonely man. The Bible can't even tell us how old Saul was when he started to rule: The number is missing.

There is something cursed about Saul, something forlorn. The real prince of his army is Samuel, not Saul. When Samuel fails to appear at a certain battle site, Saul grows frightened and offers up in sacrifice sheep and oxen he should have destroyed, as God had dictated to Samuel, and Samuel had dictated to Saul. The Lord will not forgive him. Saul can pray and grovel, but he has become like a dead man. He rules without the word of God. The Lord provides His own king, David, a young shepherd boy who is ruddy and handsome and has beautiful eyes. Yet, though Samuel anoints the boy, Saul still rules the nation.

The Lord torments him with an evil spirit, and it is only young David who can cure it. "And whenever the evil spirit from God was upon Saul, David took the lyre and played it with his hand; so Saul was refreshed, and was well, and the evil spirit departed from him" (16:23). Saul takes the shepherd boy into his service as an armor-bearer and "loved him greatly" (16:21).

Enter Goliath. The giant of Gath challenges the entire Hebrew nation. Saul shivers along with the rest of the Hebrews when Goliath stands in his armor "with greaves of brass upon his legs, and a javelin of brass between his shoulders" (17:6), and says, "I defy the ranks of Israel this day; give me a man, that we may fight together" (17:10). And David agrees to fight Goliath. What does a giant mean to David when David has already destroyed the lions and bears that threatened his flock? The miraculous shepherd boy, with Jehovah on his side, "prevailed over the Philistine with a sling and with a stone, and struck the Philistine and killed him; there was no sword in the hand of David" (17:50). The Hebrews have a new champion, and that champion isn't Saul.

> *Saul has slain his thousands,*
> *And David his ten thousands.*

> (18:7)

Thus sing the women of Israel after David destroys Goliath. Saul grows angry and "eyed David from that day on" (18:9). His destruction starts with a heartless song—spiteful *and* joyous. It's meant to belittle Saul and separate him from the boy hero who is adored by God. Saul is unadored. He was flung at the Hebrews, because they had lost faith in Jehovah. And once the Hebrew women sing, Saul is profoundly jealous. He knows that the Lord prefers this shepherd boy. Demons possess Saul. He has to seek out a witch. "God has turned away from me and answers me no more, either by prophets or by dreams" (28:15). The witch summons up the ghost of Samuel, who tells Saul that "the Lord has torn the kingdom out of your hand, and gives it to your neighbor, David" (28:17). And from that moment Saul himself is a ghost, the ghost of a king.

This is why Israel's first king haunts us like no other character in the Bible. He's as bewitched as our own century. Eaten with guilt, isolated, utterly without the Lord, he could have come out of Kafka's parables or Borges' bookish tales. I've lived with that maddened king most of my life. He sticks to my dreams.

I never much cared for David. The little giant-slayer is as competent as any Boy Scout. He has no demons to upset him. Saul's own son Jonathan protects David. He's the darling of the nation, the bringer of song. David is like a musical score. He "civilizes" the Hebrews with his lyre. His house prospers and he begets a whole line of kings. The history of Israel as a unified nation begins with the shepherd king and his lyre. And Saul dies on the battlefield with his three sons. The Philistines over-take him, as the ghost of Samuel had predicted, and the king asks his armor-bearer to "thrust me through" with his sword so that the Philistines will not "make sport of me" (31:4). But Saul's armor-bearer is too frightened to kill a king. And the king falls upon his own sword. "Thus Saul died, and his three sons, and his armor-bearer, and all his men, on the same day together" (31:6). And the house of Saul disappears.

He is a king without issue, a kind of walking shadow, a ghost boy who hides in the baggage. Saul is constantly with the night. Twice in the first book of Samuel he enters a cave to "relieve himself" (24:3) while he's hunting down David, and then in order to visit Samuel's ghost in the land of the dead. Saul's constant night turns him into a metaphorical man. He's the king of a "dark" nation that will flower under David. He lives in a dark time, without voices or visions. He serves as a sacrificial bridge that connects a primitive, warlike people with many gods and many tribes to a nation that serves one Lord, one God, with a continuous line under King David. And my own sentiments remain with Saul.

We also live in a time without voices or visions. If Jehovah sings to us, it's hard to hear. We're as deaf as King Saul. "The voice of the turtle is heard in the land, heard in all the arts—in literature, painting, and music—and in the voices of men and women speaking to one another," says John Bleibtreu in *The Parable of the Beast.*

> *It is not the voice of the dove, that sweet and melancholy sound which the translators of the Authorized Version presumably had in mind; it is the croak of isolation and alienation issuing*

from within a vault of defensive armor—the
voice of the reptilian turtle. This armor we
wear—the armor of technology separating us
from the rest of the natural world—has created
us lately in the condition of exiles. Nature exists
within as well as without, and we are become,
therefore, exiled from ourselves. The style of the
catatonic has become the style of Everyman.

Saul is this catatonic Everyman: godless, alone, with the mocking sound of the turtle in his head. We ourselves are armored like Goliath and Saul. Our entire psyches are clothed "with greaves of brass." Our ears are stuffed. We seek our own witch of Endor in the caves of art. We long for voices—to rediscover our lyric selves. But the melodies are rare.

The Renaissance adored young David. He was Florence's own adopted child. Renderings of David could be found everywhere in that powerful city-state. Michelangelo turned him into a pleasing, handsome giant—a rational Goliath with wonderful loins. But where are the renderings of Saul?

It doesn't matter how many variations, or strands, there are to 1 Samuel, palimpsests and pentimentos, earlier and later drafts. In none of them is Saul the hero. He's always melancholic, afraid to rule. He is perhaps the first schizophrenic king. Saul's *disease* is the terror of a man who's lost the voice of God. He seeks God and finds only demons. He accuses all his servants of plotting against him (22:8) and protecting David. The voices in his ear gradually darken. He doesn't even have the benefit of David's lyre. The love he felt for David turns to madness and despair. Saul's demons separate him from every other man.

He lacks David's sense of politics and song. Saul is a primitive: There is almost nothing he experiences in 1 Samuel that isn't related to fear—fear of Samuel, fear of David, fear of God, fear of Goliath and the Philistines, fear of his servants, fear of his son Jonathan. When he fails to destroy the Amalekites, and still spares their king and their cattle, Samuel rebukes him and says, "Though you are little in your own eyes, are you not the head of the tribes of Israel?" (15:17)

Saul *is* little in his own eyes, because he never wanted to become king. What could that first king have been to the tribes of Israel? Half man, half god, prophet, warrior, and magician, a substitute for Jehovah Himself. Saul was much too simple and solitary a man to play at being a god. David can kill Goliath, talk to God, and mourn the dead Saul with an eloquence that borders on the magical:

> *Ye daughters of Israel, weep over Saul,*
> *who clothed you daintily in scarlet,*
> *who put ornaments of gold upon your apparel.*

And Saul has nothing but his rages, his fears, and his own silence. He cannot pull magic out of a sling

and kill a giant for his people. Jehovah has cursed Saul
by making him king. And perhaps the most poignant
and haunted moment in 1 Samuel is connected to
Saul's isolation as a man and a king.

In this one adventure, Saul is preparing to murder
David and David's band of men. He enters a cave near
Wildgoats' Rock in order to move his bowels in private.
David himself is hiding in that cave with his men, who
beseech him to murder Saul. David does something
else. While the king squats, "David arose and stealth-
ily cut off the skirt of Saul's robe" (24:4). But David is
still the Boy Scout: "And afterward David's heart smote
him, because he had cut off Saul's skirt" (24:5). And he
will permit none of his men to harm the king.

Saul leaves the cave, and the Boy Scout runs after
him with his particular piece of evidence. "See, my
father, see the skirt of your robe in my hand; for by the
fact that I cut off the skirt of your robe, and did not
kill you, you may know and see that there is no wrong
or treason in my hands. I have not sinned against you,
though you hunt my life to take it" (24:11).

David's words are like his lyre; while he sings them,
Saul's madness flees. "'Is this your voice, my son David?'
And Saul lifted up his voice and wept. He said to David,
'you are more righteous than I; for you have repaid me
good, whereas I have repaid you evil'" (24:16–17).

There's something oddly touching about that "com-
munion" in the cave: Saul's own secret act of defecation
is secretly interrupted by David. But a bonding occurs

between the two men. The squatting king is closer to David than he will ever be, and yet he has no sense of this: he is still a king alone in the dark. His madness soon returns; he starts to hunt David all over again, and David hides among the Philistines. Samuel is dead. David is gone. And Saul's divided army destroys itself. The king and his entire house turn to dust.

2

WHO WILL CHERISH SAUL, sing his praises? No one but David. He laments the passing of Jonathan and Saul, who were "swifter than eagles" (2 Samuel 1:23). But not even David's lament can rescue Saul. Saul has few echoes beyond his own sad history, while Jonathan is remembered as the beloved friend of David.

> *I am distressed for you, my brother Jonathan;*
> *very pleasant have you been to me;*
> *your love to me was wonderful,*
> *passing the love of women.*
>
> [2 Samuel 1:26]

And if the Bible is ambiguous about Saul's age and the years of his rule, it is relentlessly clear on the subject of King David: "David was thirty years old when he began to reign, and he reigned forty years" (2 Samuel 5:4).

David is a man of many appetites, climates, and roles—lover, father, husband, soldier, poet, musician, king. He woos Bathsheba, Abigail, and Abishag, keeps a harem of wives. He conciliates, cajoles. He dances, sings, and sins. He creates a new capital. We have a city of David, a star of David ... and nothing for Saul (David had his empire, and Saul had his fits).

And yet it is through this very nothingness that we finally celebrate Saul. He has no Abishag to warm his bed. His son Ish-bosheth succeeds him for a while and is murdered by his own two captains (and David swallows the house of Saul). We have no music to remember him by. He exists in the hollows, in the spaces around his kingdom, in the empty designs of his rule. Negativity and narrowness are his earmarks, the tags of Saul. He is the king who gives way to David, like the howls and birth pangs of a nation. Saul is that ambiguous line where history begins.

While David is in hiding, he establishes his covenant with the dispossessed. "And every one who was in distress, and every one who was in debt, and everyone who was discontented, gathered to him" (22:2). And that's how he collects an empire and an army. But Saul consorts with witches, demons, and ghosts. He's king of the impalpable, of those things that cannot be touched. David is the builder of cities and words, the poet-prince. He is rational and sane and devious, the perfect Boy Scout. Saul is insane, or irrational at least. If he could have disguised his own terror, he might have used David as a spear against the Philistines. But the king's at war ... with himself. He loves David,

fears David, is jealous of David, and cannot negoti-
ate among his feelings and moods. He'd prefer to deal
with David's ghost rather than David.

After Samuel dies, Saul puts "the mediums and
the wizards out of the land" (28:3). But he's afraid of
the Philistines. He shucks off the garments of a king
and visits the witch of Endor. He enters her "cave." He
asks her to bring Samuel up out of the cave, the same
Samuel who anointed and abandoned Saul. What
good news could a dead prophet bring? Samuel had no
love for Saul. Yet the king persists. In a deaf time, he
needs to hear a prophet.

The ghost is angry at him. "Why have you disturbed
me by bringing me up?" (28:15)

Saul doesn't shiver before this ghost of Samuel
"wrapped in a robe" (28:14). He has summoned Samuel so that Samuel can tell him what to do. The ghost
answers: "Why then do you ask me, since the Lord
has turned from you and become your enemy?" (28:16)
"Tomorrow," the ghost says, "you and your sons shall
be with me" (28:19).

The king falls to the ground. The ghost departs. The
witch of Endor feeds Saul. And the next day, after the
Philistine archers surround Saul and wound him, the
king falls upon his sword.

Thus Saul's story ends: the reluctant king who fell
out of grace with the Lord. "There was not a man among
the people of Israel more handsome than he" (9:2). But
Saul's handsomeness wasn't enough. His very selection

ruins him. He was a little too handsome, a little too tall. And it's the awfulness of his fate—the king as doomed man—that moves the modern reader.

Our own lives seem as arbitrary as Saul's. The blessing of his kingship was only another form of curse. In a century of mass migration and mass murder, of dreamlike poverty and dreamlike wealth, of businessmen-philosophers and pauper-kings, Saul seems as familiar as our own brooding face.

> *Saul has slain his thousands,*
> *And David his ten thousands.*

If David is history's darling, then we, all the modern fools—liars, jugglers, wizards without song—still have Saul.

Ellis: An Autobiography
(1986)

1

BRONX BOY, I GREW UP in a poor man's pile of streets, a ghetto called Morrisania, which had its own Black Belt on Boston Road and a strip of bodegas under the tracks of Southern Boulevard, a wall of Irish surrounding Crotona Park, and a heartland of Italians and Jews, poor as hell, except for a handful of furriers, accountants, lonely physicists, and our congressman, who lived on Crotona Park East, something of a golden corridor, with courtyards facing a long stitch of green. This congressman was supposed to have an idiot son who'd seen *The Mark of Zorro* too many times and haunted his own building with cape and sword, coming out from behind the banisters to challenge housewives and delivery boys to a duel. It could have been an apocryphal tale. But one of the delivery boys was a friend of mine. I didn't invent the scar on his face. He'd been touched by Zorro. But it's the nature of politics that our congressman's son was never carted off to an asylum. The

49

corridors and the stairwell were his particular paradise. Perhaps it wasn't corruption on the part of Congress, or even political pull. Just simple neighborliness that allowed Zorro to lumber in the halls. Golden corridor or not, it was still a ghetto, and the ghetto protected its own. Naturally, these were romantic times (circa 1948), before there was ever a South Bronx.

The Bronx I remember consisted of east and west. The official demarcation line was Jerome Avenue. But Jerome Avenue was so far to the west that most of the Bronx remained in some deep pit, an endless east that was like a continent. And so we made our own geographer's rules. The Bronx's Champs Elysées, known as the Grand Concourse, became our magic marker. Everything near the Concourse was considered west. When you arrived at the bottom of Claremont Park, you were in no-man's-land, that hazy border where the East Bronx began. By the time you got to Third Avenue, there was no longer any doubt: you'd entered the borough's eastern heart, land of the lower middle class.

Morrisania was where Ed Koch was born. And if our mayor seems rambunctious, it's nothing more than the heritage of Crotona Park. If he moved to Jersey by the time he was eight, so what? Eight's an old man. Ed Koch was formed by Crotona Park and Boston Road. He was always a street kid, a kind of Bronx savage. And he runs our city with a savage's code of honor. "I'm not the type to get ulcers. I give them," he says. He's Ivan the Terrible with a Bronx lisp. A wild child, like me.

That's where the resemblance ends. I'm the one with ulcers. I was something of a thief. I swiped polo shirts and pink erasers. I hustled chess on the rooftops and in the streets, shoving pawns down my sleeve when an opponent's eye would stray. I twitched a lot, like some casualty of a long-forgotten war. I walked the streets like a city wolf, eyeing, eyeing everything. My father rarely worked. He existed in a state of psychic grief. I couldn't grasp his syllables when he talked. There was some horrible undeclared war between us.

I was a guerrilla in my father's house. I lived under siege in the room I shared with my brother. But I wasn't Maxim Gorky or Kerouac. I couldn't take to the road. I wore my swaddling clothes a terribly long time. Illiterate as I was, without a dictionary at home, I became a Talmudic scholar, seeking revenge on my father with words. The only library in Morrisania was on the black side of Boston Road. I crossed into that ghetto, the lone white wolf, to borrow a child's life of Spinoza. That little glass grinder was a revelation to me. He defied all the Jewish patriarchs of old Amsterdam to declare that the universe was outside Jehovah's jurisdiction. He compared it to a giant clock, subject to musical and mathematical laws. Spinoza ground his glass in isolation, and I suffered over his story, a child in the New Amsterdam of the Bronx. But I wasn't so successful with my dad. I belittled him in Spinoza's voice, talked of clockworks in the sky (I was twelve), and he beat me with a broom.

That was thirty-six years ago, and I've developed

amnesia about my dad. Had to or I couldn't have survived. But I never really rubbed away that relentless look of anger in his eye, as if my existence were an affront to him, an outrage he had to endure. That's how my twitch began. It was like an electrical scream running through my body, my own musical clock, filled with fury. I was Spinoza's planet of storms. I've buried that twitch somewhere, but how do you find the right cost accounting to compensate for the anger of your own dad? He's seventy-five. His hair is blacker than mine. I still can't understand his syllables. He speaks a language of wounds. His New Amsterdam wasn't very kind to him. A Polish boy, he'd come to America all by himself. His mother had left him behind in the Old World because he suffered from conjunctivitis. He lived with an aunt near Warsaw until his pinkeye was cured. Ah, but was it ever cured? My father carried it with him to America, like a mark on the brain. I never once saw him smile at his mother or his father, who'd arrived earliest of all and sold apples in sweatshops and on the streets. That was my grandfather's single success: apples for every season of the year. No spectacular rise. No great drama. Just a railroad flat on Henry Street in Manhattan and a history of apples.

I sought prouder tales, like *The Rise of David Levinsky,* the metamorphosis of my grandfather into a merchant prince. Or a bit of a gangster maybe. Couldn't he have cornered the market on apples, parceled out the supply, like cocaine? It would have given me pleasure to brag of my grandfather as the Lower East Side's apple king. But that's infantile romance. My grandfather was an apple peddler with yellow teeth and no English in his skull. At least my father graduated to a sewing machine. He had a talent for building fur coats. That talent wasn't much prized after World War II. A recession hit the country, my father went into business for himself, bought a car. It almost seemed as if he'd solved the riddle of the United States, becoming the owner of a Plymouth and an entrepreneur. The car was my security blanket. I can still recall the emblem on its hood, that silver reproduction of a ship, the *Mayflower*'s little shining masts. My father had produced his own Plymouth Rock. He was a Polish Pilgrim with a fur cutter's knife.

I dreamt of my father's Plymouth, green and silver, with wood paneling and straw upholstery, my dad and I both at the wheel, sailing over Crotona Park into the outlands of Riverdale, like a long creamy ride to the moon. But that Plymouth never got us out of the East Bronx. It sat in its garage most of the time. My father never learned to drive. His business failed. He sold the car and sank into debt. His Pilgrim days were over. We landed in poverty and were anchored there. It terrified me. From the day I entered high school, I was never sure we'd have enough to eat. My father would go down to the fur market and sit behind a machine for a month or two. His work was as seasonal as selling apples in the street.

I buried my nose in report cards. I was the Talmudic prince, too involved in academics to find a part-time job. I could always defeat my father by grabbing A's and B's. I wondered why he never abandoned us, left to start another life. His rage seemed so incredibly large. But he was stuck in some seesaw battle with himself, a battle I couldn't understand. He'd remained my mother's child, angry from the minute he woke to the minute he started to snore.

I went on to college, but I still lived at home. Became a substitute teacher in the city's school system, like a wandering minstrel, going from school to school with Spinoza's bag of tricks. I talked about the universe—the possibility of planets like our own, with a duplicate Bronx and ghettos of green men. I was adored by most of my students, Mr. C., the "sub" who softened Shakespeare with science fiction.

I got married, moved to California. The marriage didn't last. I was caught in the middle of a war zone I'd created. I was still that savage from Crotona Park, a golem who'd been building my own feet of clay, without a magical rabbi to protect me, as the original golem had—some medieval man who might give me lessons in diplomacy and manners. I drifted from relationship to relationship, unable to settle in long enough to have a child. Golems aren't such terrific mates. We're too busy sucking clay.

I was haunted, like that congressman's son, old Zorro, but I didn't attack people in apartment houses. I had a much more reasonable career. I taught college, I wrote books, but I was still a golem, cradled in some unreasonable fear.

And then, by luck, I happened to start a novel about a Polish gangster who'd gone through Ellis in 1900, and I wanted to see what that island was all about. Bought a ticket at Battery Park, climbed aboard a little ferry with a bundle of tourists, and we landed on the corroded docks of the old immigrant station. The station looked like a Polish castle lost in the weeds. The roofs had bite marks in them, as if they'd been under attack from some prehistoric bird.

A U.S. ranger took us on a guided trip through the main building. That ranger knew her facts. She was a woman of twenty-five or six, with trousers, a military buckle, and a ranger's hat. She talked of the baggage room, where immigrants had to store their belongings when they got to Ellis, the Isle of Tears. She didn't lecture in a condescending way. She showed us the dining room, where immigrants could eat for less than a dime in 1910. The walls were cracked. The floor had begun to buckle. Nothing was tarted up for us. No fancy paint or an added bench. The whole bloody island was in disrepair. The station had been closed for a long time. The United States couldn't seem to get rid of it. There'd been some talk of turning it into a gambling casino. But Lyndon Johnson, who was president when that rumor hit, wouldn't donate Ellis Island to a syndicate of gamblers. That's what the ranger told us.

She took us step by step through an immigrant's day, and for me it was like going through the Stations of the Cross, rituals of suffering every five or ten feet.

Immigrants had to climb a flight of stairs while doctors looked at them and chalked up their clothes with secret signs, a cabalistic code that recorded whether they had tuberculosis, suffered from pinkeye, or had suspicious lumps. I imagined myself being plucked by foreign hands and shouted at in a language that must have sounded like all the babble of the world. I was thrilled and scared, a voyeur passing through my mother and father's primal journey to America.

We arrived at the Great Hall, the enormous registry room where immigrants were processed and tagged. It was a tall cave with a barreled roof. It had a bridge along the sides where relatives might wait, or some chief inspector could look down at the proceedings. Nothing had prepared me for the deep well of that room, the accumulation of so much emptied space. Great pendulous chandeliers with missing globes lent a kind of sadness to the room. But they couldn't mask the awfulness of that place, like some Roman arena for horses to prance, horses and slaves.

No one could have felt secure in a room like that, big as America. I would have crapped in my pants. Not from fear of the processing station, but from the hopelessness of a room where you could no longer define yourself. Grandfathers, pregnant women, criminals could only have shivered and behaved like a child.

Seventeen million people went through that station. My father was only one man. But I understood his pathology for the first time. He'd never quite recovered from Ellis Island. Yes, yes, he'd been damaged before all that. No pathology can begin in some registry room. But I'd swear the island had stunned him, chalked my father for life. An odd case? Perhaps. Others got through it, went on to brilliant careers. But I wonder if Ellis Island didn't leave some invisible tag.

It's dangerous to impose one person's psychic dilemma upon the history of a whole town. The Big Apple had been around over 250 years before that station was ever built. But I still believe that *modern* New York comes right out of Ellis Island.

That argument may be the prejudice of an immigrant boy, but it's also a perfect hook to comprehend a city that's so varied, so dense, that contradicts itself minute by minute, the most European of all American cities and the most American of any city in the world. In 1975, people thought New York would become another Atlantis and disappear into the ocean. The city had to beg money to keep alive from day to day. It couldn't meet its enormous payroll. Our mayor, a five-foot-three accountant who'd come from the Brooklyn machine, was ignored by almost everyone. The wounded hippopotamus of New York stumbled around old Abraham Beame. Abe had to fire people. But the wounded hippo couldn't even tell how many people were on its payroll. Companies scattered across the river. An investment banker, Felix Rohatyn, formed a kind of shadow government. He was our Cromwell, saving us and reducing us, like an animal doctor who can heal a hippopotamus. Rohatyn ran New York. He brokered for every group, obliged our unions to swallow the city's "paper," bonds that no one wanted to buy. The city had to decimate its services. Teachers, firemen, and cops were let go. Playgrounds became shadowlands. Central Park grew dirty and wild. The Bronx was burning. Most construction had stopped. Manhattan was beginning to look like a phantom village.

Ten years later, New York is the acknowledged capital of the world. The hippo has come out of its own big sleep. Henry Kissinger lives here now. We have Trump Tower and Philip Johnson's AT&T. We have a whole city within a city being built near Battery Park. You can see blue pyramids rising out of the rock piles. Manhattan is becoming a fairyland of new construction. It has its own Ramblas on Columbus Avenue, where mannequins look like real people, and customers in restaurants and ice-cream parlors remind you of dummies in a window. The Bronx has stopped burning. We have ranch houses in the rubble of Charlotte Street, and the Grand Concourse is being rehabbed, block by block. Brownsville is still Berlin, but Bed-Stuy is beginning to look like Greenwich Village. The Big Apple has become a boomtown under Ed Koch. Traveling with him one afternoon, I watched his gray eyes peer at a houseboat moored to a city dock. "I don't know who owns this houseboat," he said, "but I'm sure they're paying rent. With me, you gotta pay rent."

You have to pay the piper, Ed Koch. The city's

coffers are high again. That Brooklyn accountant, Abe Beame, is long gone from City Hall, and a king rules there now, a street king who loves eggplant and garlic sauce and brings his own brown bag to Italian restaurants. We come from similar clay, but I'm prepared to argue all his policies, while I sit in the mayor's limousine. His own adviser, Dan Wolf, had invited me to have lunch with the street king.

"Mr. Mayor . . . "

His gray eyes swiveled out. "Call me Ed."

"We went to the same school. We're practically citizens of Crotona Park. Only what about—"

"The death penalty," he says, like a wizard who can anticipate my words. "Capital punishment is not extreme. Torture would be extreme."

The wizard disarmed me before I could declare my case. The lunch turns into an endless picnic because Koch lets me follow him around for the rest of the day. It's June 1985, and the mayor has declared a moratorium on politics. He basks in golden silence. Koch won't campaign, except for his flurry of press conferences, often twice a day. Everybody knows that he'll win the primary with a whisper or two.

The Irish were becoming his most loyal constituency. He had 81 percent of the Irish vote. The Italians were next in line, with almost 80 percent.

"What about the Jews?" I asked.

A bit of gray went out of his eyes. "Seventy-three percent," he said, as if he'd been mugged in Gracie

Mansion. Then he laughed, and his eyes broke into their usual color. "Gives me an opportunity to say the Jews are a little crazy."

We didn't have to talk about the Protestant vote. The WASPs were like some forgotten country in New York politics. In spite of its sudden renaissance, New York still hadn't climbed out of the melting pot. The Yuppies might rule on Columbus Avenue, but the Irish and Italians would deliver the vote. There were over three million Catholics in the city of New York.

I rode in a helicopter with Koch to Riverdale. Our heliport was near the wonderful old fire station in Battery Park. "It will be turned into a restaurant," the mayor told me. He put on metal earmuffs. "I have a problem with my ears."

The chopper lifted off the ground, close to the Statue of Liberty and her latticed truss, all that scaffolding to prepare for her hundredth birthday in America. I watched the blue curl of the water under our feet. Ellis Island looked like a bit of candied grass and stone. It couldn't have traumatized a horsefly from up here. But I wasn't fooled by a helicopter's slanting run. That station still stood in the ruined grass, a reminder of who we were and where we'd come from, even if it hadn't housed immigrants in over forty years. We landed in a baseball field, the police chopper bumping down onto the grass. The neighborhood kids were in awe of Ed Koch, a king who'd come out of the sky, and I was the king's apprentice. The kids waved to all of Koch's retinue, bodyguards and advance men. He was going to deliver the commencement address at the Riverdale Country School. He'd slept on the chopper, glanced at the notes of his speech. Koch is notorious for inventing his own speeches. He's as quick as Lenny Bruce, but this street king has an instinct for survival. He's the greatest stand-up comic City Hall has ever had.

But the mayor decided not to be funny in Riverdale. I stood behind the podium with the mayor's bodyguards, amid a fairyland of clean white faces. The bodyguards laughed among themselves. One of them was black. "They charge a special rate for blacks," he said. "It's twice as expensive for blacks to get in."

Public service was "the noblest of professions" for Ed Koch. He'd written a best-seller, diminishing presidents, governors, and a few mayors, but that gave him no "psychic satisfaction," he said. "I love my job. Everybody knows that. If you don't, I'm telling you now." The street king isn't descended from a royal line of mayors. He's a mongrel, like the rest of us. "My parents were immigrants from Poland," he said. And the Apple was unique because "sons and daughters of immigrants could rise so high and so quickly. . . . There are very few places where that is so."

As we left the grounds of the school, a student approached Koch. He didn't look like a wacko. The bodyguards let him through. He had a curious picture for the mayor to sign. He'd once been photographed with Koch, but the photographer had "lost" him and captured only his hand. The student wanted Koch to sign that disembodied hand in the photograph. This encounter could have been a piece of fiction, a parable out of Kafka, but the mayor didn't hesitate for a moment. He scribbled his name over the hand and we returned to the helicopter.

There was an ambulance on either side of the chopper. The mayor winked. "One ambulance for each of us." The dust spread around us as we walked to the chopper, climbed a tiny stool, sat down, belted ourselves in at the back of the machine, the mayor giving his thumbs-up sign to a crowd of kids near the ball field, that magical king who had dropped down into their territory in an iron bird, and rose up out of their lives. I congratulated him on his speech.

"Ah," he said. "I was bored. My heart wasn't in it."

But he'd told my tale, an immigrant story. He was just another Polish boy, riding into the wind. It didn't matter that all the property around him was his. It was on loan to him as mayor. In New York only a public servant could become king. Donald Trump had his name in gold on a building; he could even construct a castle with a moat on Lexington or Third, but he'd never preside over Gracie Mansion, no matter how many millions he had. Koch wasn't king for life; it was only a borrowed mansion. But he'd made New York his by the force of his personality; he'd imposed himself upon the town.

The streets of Riverdale looked like cardboard cutouts. We rode back into the city's heart; the Manhattan skyline was like an ugly toyland of similar cluttered boxes, rescued only by the Chrysler Building and its eccentric silver top. We climbed down toward the piers and bounced onto the heliport's floor. The mayor removed his metal earmuffs and we ran to his car. He was already late for his next speech.

2

MY DAY WITH KOCH FELT LIKE A TAPESTRY off the rotting walls of Ellis Island. The sons of immigrants out on a ride. But it was more than that. The mayor had no dinner plans, and he invited me back to Gracie Mansion after one of his marathon town hall meetings. He'd fielded questions for an hour and a half. It was brutal work. Everyone in the audience seemed to have a grievance against New York. Koch didn't shirk. He had no slick answers. He'd involved himself in some intimate dance with the audience. If soccer players were pissing outside a woman's window, Koch guaranteed that they would no longer piss. One old man complained, "I've been mugged so often, if I'm not mugged, I feel the muggers are angry at me."

The mayor didn't rattle off crime statistics to that old man or try to snow him with facts and figures. He conferred with the deputy police commissioner at his side and told the man, "We'll follow it up. Let me tell you."

He created "marriages" at this meeting, putting people together with his commissioners, having the commissioners promise to look at local problems out on the street. A certain Mrs. Moskowitz could hardly believe it when Koch invited a deputy sanitation commissioner to sit down with her the next day and examine the garbage problems on her block. "I'll have coffee with you," she told the commissioner.

The mayor said, "I'll be back," and I followed him out of the auditorium with his bodyguards. We took the chopper back to Manhattan. I was becoming a sky cowboy: four helicopter rides in one day. We landed at a Pan Am heliport on the East River, and I rode with the mayor to his mansion.

Koch was beat. His schedule would break an ordinary man. He was on the go from six in the morning to midnight. He had "opened" City Hall at seven-thirty, and now I sat with him in his living room at Gracie Mansion, eating pasta and lamb chops and drinking red wine.

We both had our dinner off a tray, watched *Reilly, Ace of Spies* and then the news, which told of a construction crew chief who earned $400,000 a year. "I work twenty-four hours a day," the crew chief said. "I'm always on call."

"A gonif," Koch said, biting into his strawberry tart.

It was time for me to go. I thanked the mayor. It was my first meal as a guest of the city. Koch dialed his chauffeur. "I have a customer for you," he said.

The mayor accompanied me to the door, slouching a little at six one. Who knows how many phone calls he had to make? He might be up in the sky again within the hour if one of his policemen was shot in some corner of Brooklyn. He was the watchman of New York. There'd been no other mayor like him before.

3

ED KOCH IS THE GOLEM MAYOR. His clay was formed on Ellis Island. His fierceness and his humor come from the Big Apple's odd split: New York has taken on a kind of schizophrenia in the twentieth century, a curious, biting wound that has little to do with the gap between rich and poor. That gap was there three hundred years ago.

Maybe we ought to examine our preschizophrenic past. The Apple's industry began with the Dutch, merchants who wouldn't allow religion to wreck a good deal. Peter Stuyvesant hated the Jews and wanted to rid them from New Amsterdam. He was the city's first anti-Semite. But the Dutch West India Company wouldn't let Peter have his way. Some of the Jews prospered, others remained poor, while New Amsterdam developed into a mercantile town.

Then the English came along, and the Dutch surrendered New Amsterdam to a tiny fleet of warships on September 8, 1664. A curious amnesia settled in for over a hundred years. How many schoolboys can recall the name of a single English governor? It's almost as if history stopped after the congenial Dutch. But we can always remember the two Peters, Stuyvesant and Minuit.

Stuyvesant was a tyrannical son of a bitch. Yet the city has a plaque where Stuyvesant's pear tree once stood. That tree outlived Stuyvesant by two hundred years.

But the English couldn't engender a single myth. It's part of our stubbornness. We've held on to our Dutch beginnings and shed our English skin.

The city seems to recapture its memory around the time of the Revolution and the English occupation of New York. It was seven years of shame, but not because of the British troops garrisoned here. The population began to swell with Loyalists. New York was Tory town, the king's own capital of the New World. The city prospered. With so many Tories, merchants, and soldiers, New York suffered its first housing shortage. Quick fortunes were made. Prices jumped over the moon. Some people had to live in tents. The town was overrun with whores, who serviced King George's Hessian and British troops, while captured American soldiers lay starving in prison ships.

Then the English lost the war and fifteen thousand Tories suddenly disappeared from sight. The city's brokers had been trading under a buttonwood tree near 68 Wall Street, but New York became the banking capital of America after this stock exchange moved indoors. Alexander Hamilton and Aaron Burr started their own banks. Hamilton was my first hero. Short, dark, with wooly hair, he was the bastard son of a Jewish merchant, Lavein or Levine. His real dad was a highborn drifter, James Hamilton. His mother, Rachel Lavein, was a bit of a whore. I always had a suspicion that other fathers were involved. Rachel Lavein had a closetful of beaux in the West Indies, where she lived. For me, young Hamilton was black *and* Jewish. He fought a duel with Aaron Burr, who wanted to become emperor of the United States, and Hamilton got himself killed. Burr became a pariah after the duel. He died in a rooming house.

He'd also been a sachem of Tammany Hall. Tammany was a narrow club of American patriots, with little regard for the Irish or any other immigrants until these native sons scratched their heads and discovered that the common tribe of landless white males suddenly had the vote. Then Tammany kissed the Irish, who'd been treated like dogs up to then, and a unique kind of politics began. Tammany helped the Irish become citizens and counted on their vote. It was the party of the rabble. And the Irish, who were used by the Tammany pols as their own donkey force, soon took over Tammany itself, and that was the beginning of modern New York, because it was the first time that a foreign rabble had competed with the "nativists" and won. "There were sixty or seventy years when the Irish were everywhere," Daniel Patrick Moynihan tells us in *Beyond the Melting Pot*. "The Irish came to run the police force *and* the underworld; they were the reformers and the hoodlums; employers and employed."

I hated the Irish as a boy. They ringed Crotona Park and wouldn't allow a little kike to enter their zones. But we all owe an enormous debt to the Irish. They helped create the character of New York, its reputation as an immigrant town. They lived in the worst rookeries when they arrived. They were exploited, beaten, forced to grub, these shanty Irish who'd grown wild and coarse under English rule and developed their own wild English, a crusty tongue that was almost like an act of vengeance upon their rulers.

The Irish came here and discovered another ruling class: politicians, bankers, and grocers. The natives clamored to send them back to Ireland, organizing into secret societies like the Order of the Star-Spangled Banner and other Know-Nothings, who were a kind of northern Klan. The Know-Nothings didn't want these wild men around, a dirty, stinking folk that never washed or combed their ruddy hair. They multiplied like rats in their stinking warrens. An Irish woman wasn't satisfied until she was delivered of thirteen sons, the Know-Nothings said. The Irish were nothing more than Negroes with white skin. They had to live among the blacks. A decent landlord wouldn't take them in. But the Know-Nothings couldn't destroy the Irish, who kept to their rookeries. The worst gangs New York has ever had were formed in the Irish slums of Mulberry Bend.

The gangs worked for Tammany, getting votes and building bonfires on election eve. The Irish legitimized themselves through their finagling and their own brute force, capturing a third of the·city vote by 1855, with their ruddy hair and dirty faces.

And when the Italians and the Jews began to arrive

from Eastern Europe after 1880, they were no more
dirty than the Irish had been. Other nativists opposed
this "eastern horde." But the Italians and Jews moved
into the old Irish rookeries on the Lower East Side.
And my granddad, who couldn't howl a word of English, became a citizen through Irish auspices. He ped-
dled his apples and voted the Tammany line. I ought
to know. I'd never have gotten born without the Irish.
My dad arrived after the National Origins Act of 1924
cut off immigration from Eastern Europe. He couldn't
have landed in America if his own dad hadn't become
a "cousin" of Tammany Hall. And Ellis Island wouldn't
have been the birthplace that bloomed in my head.

4

ELLIS WAS AN ISLAND THAT NO ONE seemed to want.
It had its particular ghosts. The Dutch called it Little
Oyster Island, but they wouldn't start a settlement there.
The English considered using it as a "pesthouse" for
victims of the plague. But even such victims couldn't
get onto the island. It was turned into a "hospital" for
pirates who were hung in Washington Market, then
rowed out to the island and chained to a gibbet. These
dead men were the island's chief inhabitants for most of
the eighteenth century. It fell into the hands of someone named Samuel Ellis, but he couldn't dispose of the
island. In 1794, Ellis's island was given to the state of
New York, and a fort was put up to house a company of

soldiers. But these men began to desert. They couldn't tolerate the loneliness of that island. New York offered it to the United States, and the island took a melancholy turn, holding British prisoners during the War of 1812. It was soon deserted again, except for an occasional hanging. Ellis couldn't seem to get away from the dead. It was a ghostly fort, staffed from time to time by the army and the navy. The navy built a powder magazine there in 1835. But that magazine wasn't much of a success. In 1861, the island had a population of five people.

Local pols began to worry about the munitions dump. One Jersey congressman calculated that if lightning ever struck the island, Hoboken, Jersey City, "and parts of New York" would disappear. But nothing happened. The dump remained on Ellis Island.

In 1882, Congress passed a bill forbidding lunatics, paupers, and convicts from entering the United States. Until then, the states themselves "determined the desirability of immigrants," according to Thomas Dunne in his text on Ellis Island. "Beginning in the 1880's . . . recurrent newspaper and magazine stories told of degenerate aliens being cast out of European and Asian alms houses, insane asylums and prisons, and dumped on the shores of America."

Congress had to choose between Ellis and Bedloe's Island (home of the Statue of Liberty) as the headquarters of a permanent screening station, but the press imagined immigrants who might leak out of the station and bother people visiting the statue and its little park.

So that former gibbet, an island of pirates and ghosts, hardly ever occupied for 250 years, was filled with "hundreds of workmen" in 1891, laboring "at a large, three story reception center, a hospital for ill and quarantined immigrants, a laundry, boiler house and electric generating plant," made of Georgia pine.

Ellis Island opened on the very first day of 1892. *Harper's Weekly* likened it to "a latter-day watering place hotel," a hotel that could process ten thousand immigrants in a single afternoon. But *Harper's* "water palace" burned down in 1897.

Immigrants were shunted to Castle Clinton, an older depot at the Battery, until Ellis Island was rebuilt as an elaborate fireproof dormitory, designed by the young architectural firm of Boring & Tilton. It was a Beaux-Arts assembly modeled after the Gare Montparnasse— immigrant house as railroad station, with a great hall of Guastavino tile. Once again, the praise was considerable. Immigrants would enter the United States in a kind of secular church with high vaulted ceilings and almost religious sunlight. The new Ellis Island was a brick and tile palace-church that could offer "lavish hospitality." Because in spite of its "nativists," America itself had become a receiving station. It was a country that had no rational order of population. It was created by other people's drifts: Dutch, French, English, Irish. . . .

In 1900, the nation's crucible was New York. Whether immigrants moved on to Milwaukee or Kalamazoo, for the vast majority of them their initial point of entry was the station at Ellis Island. The processing usually took about four hours. *Four hours,* and I've become the bard of trouble, singing about lifetime wounds. Battle scars, victimization. I'm not searching for a sentimental paradigm of failure, a bleeding heart. Most of the immigrants came through Ellis and went on to form their own character. Their fate wasn't determined by Ellis Island unless they were ill or were "troublemakers" sent back to Europe on the "anarchists' boat." Indeed, there were three thousand suicides on Ellis Island, sometimes more than six a month. Most of these weren't the result of that simple march up the stairs to the registry room. The men, women, and children who committed suicide were detainees, those who were kept on the island and weren't allowed "in." But I'm talking about that *investment* each immigrant must have made, fathers, mothers, bachelor women and men thrusting themselves into the New World; the hallucinatory image they held in their minds during days of steerage, *land of gold, land of gold,* and the residual fear that America wouldn't take them, no matter how healthy they were *or* unpolitical. The fear must have passed: only 2 percent didn't make it, the lungers and the anarchists, midgets and known murderers.

And the others? Seventeen million souls. I'd be willing to bet my life that most of them didn't *lose* Ellis Island, that in some piece of their psyche they were always "five minutes out of steerage." Ellis was still a ghost island. The babble they'd heard went deep. That didn't prevent them from becoming farmers in

Wisconsin or gravitating to the Lower East Side, an infinite ghetto land that could swallow greenhorns looking for patches of Europe on Grand Street, particularly if those greenhorns were Italians and Jews. Peasants for the most part, they'd felt betrayed by all the czars and kings that ruled them. They didn't take kindly to governments. The Sicilians who came here were considered savages by the rest of Italy, "black Italians." And the Russian and Polish Jews, with their beards and wigs and funny hats, were a planet apart from the uptown German Jews, those who'd arrived long before Ellis and had established themselves as brokers and department-store tycoons, and prayed in temples that were the closest thing to a Protestant church.

The downtown Jews clung to their ghettos, sold apples, like my granddad, or grew much more ambitious. Some became tycoons like the uptown temple-goers. But they had the authentic stink of the street. And a sadness. It wasn't simply a conflict of the Old World and the New, the shedding of phylacteries for a button-down collar. It was the sheer explosion of their lives, the replication upon replication of immigrant tales, like looking at your double in the window, a double with dark lines on his or her face. The Jews had fled from Czar Nicholas and his thirty-year induction policy, which made a soldier out of you from kindergarten to the grave. Grand Street had no pogroms. But it was futile to consider yourself part of a black-coated colony. This was New York, a town that had just swallowed up four other boroughs, absorbed Coney Island and Forest Hills.

In 1880, twenty years before the appearance of Ellis Island's brick church, there were less than 100,000 Jews in New York, a quiet population that had no criminal class. Hardly a single murder had ever been committed by a Jew in the United States, from the time of the Dutch through the English rule and a hundred years of independence. There'd even been a banker-patriot, Haym Salomon, a refugee from Poland, who'd helped finance the Revolutionary War. I ought to know. Haym Salomon haunted my childhood. He'd come to my public school in a film featuring Claude Rains. He was a pious man, singing in a prayer shawl and doing undercover work for the Sons of Liberty. But Claude Rains was also the Phantom of the Opera, a devil with an acid-eaten face who lived in the scaffolding above *La Bohème* and murdered opera people. That's the misfortune of movies. Actors never stick to one role. Haym Salomon was the Phantom of the Opera and Claude Rains. That Phantom terrorized me. I couldn't go to the toilet in peace. And in my own immature mind, an evil man in a black hat had saved the Revolution and started the United States.

But Haym Salomon died long before the mass immigration of Jews. In 1900, there were 600,000 of us in New York, packed into the Lower East Side, which had become a Jewish Calcutta. Those with a little more wealth or wanderlust had already gone up to Harlem or established colonies in the new borough of Brooklyn. By 1910, the Jewish population had doubled to twelve hundred thousand and Brownsville was a second Lower East Side. There was also a considerable cadre of Jewish whores and thieves. In *World of Our Fathers*, Irving Howe dismisses this cadre as a kind of growing pain, some simple disorder of the dispossessed: ". . . crime was a marginal phenomenon," he tells us, "a pathology discoloring the process of collective assertion and adjustment."

I can guarantee Irving Howe that the assertion wasn't so collective in the Bronx. And this was forty years after 1910. In the lower depths of Morrisania, at the edges of Charlotte Street, Jewish gangs flourished with their Italian counterparts long before that great blitz of the 1970s, when even the rats were organized into gangs, because the burnt-out buildings had thrown them onto the rubble with wild dogs.

But there were no wild dogs in 1950. Humans could still venture into Crotona Park, sit around Indian Lake, which hadn't grown into a rotting swamp. But we were the poorest Jews in creation. Progress had passed us by. Our fathers hadn't gone to City College, that Harvard of Harlem Heights, which was supposed to be 90 percent Jewish. City College graduates didn't come to Morrisania. We were the lumpen, lumpen proletariat, Jews that were left behind.

We still had one foot on Ellis Island, though I couldn't have known that as a boy. We were the underside of that Jewish success story—the leap from Ellis

Island to dentistry school in one lousy generation. There were enough Jewish dentists around to pack the Polo Grounds. But what did that mean to us? My father never had a checking account. I knew what checks were. I'd read Theodore Dreiser. But I had a savings booklet, like my dad. It was my wife who introduced me to the magic of scribbling checks.

I was a greenhorn without ever realizing it. Morrisania was one big registry room. My brother Harvey's a greenhorn, too. Took him fifty years to feel comfortable riding in a plane. He was a terrific puncher as a kid. The Irish would have owned all of Crotona Park if it hadn't been for my brother Harvey. He's a homicide detective, and I'd swear he doesn't have a checking account. Talk to me about the "lightning leap" of Jews. Harvey's son is a cop, like him. And if I had a son, he'd be an apple peddler.

And my dad? He's still caught in the daze of Ellis Island. A ghost without a gibbet tree. He's been enduring this country like a complicated dream. I wouldn't have uncovered his muteness in America without my own research trip to that island. Ellis was his teacher, Ellis showed him how to talk. He had a wolf's call, a howling that passed for English. I'd taught myself to grasp the lines in his face, not the words, but the little puckers of need. My father wasn't a frigging cryptogram. If I'd had his pinkeye and was kept in Warsaw with an aunt, I'd have stood under the Guastavino vaults and howled a song that held to no continent, but was a general closing down, a shutting off of the engine. It didn't matter. I'd inherited my father's muteness: the very act of writing is only a mute's revenge on a talkative world.

That's modern New York, a mixture of silence and screams. It's a city with no sound barriers. Noises echo everywhere and boom back into silence. We golems have imposed ourselves upon the contours of New York. Pathology has a way of seeming normal in this town. Think of Yannick Noah, tennis champion and former refugee from France. After he won the French Open in 1983, Noah fell apart. Paris became his personal blitz. People wouldn't leave him alone. Interview followed interview, until his insides ripped. He walked Paris like a zombie in the middle of the night and considered suicide. But Noah didn't jump off any bridge.

He landed in New York. He could chew on a bagel in SoHo without reporters sitting near his knee. Noah was anonymous in New York. "I can wear what I want to wear, be however I want to be, feel free in the middle of people. You can even scream, and nobody cares because everybody is screaming," he confessed to Jane Gross of *The New York Times*.

That's what New York is, a howling in the head, a great babble of voices, like a siren's song, the screams of Ellis Island. This is the one city in the world where communities explode and die with such regularity, they aren't noticed at all. I dare anyone to track the path of Russian and Polish Jews in New York and discover a rational line. It's almost as if a flight mechanism is built into our bones. The Grand Concourse was *our* boulevard, the most ordered, stable Jewish society, all through the 1950s; by 1978, it was almost a Mayan ruin. Apologists will say that sons and daughters ran to the suburbs and that the old were frightened of a "black invasion" from the East Bronx. But it was much more than that, a kind of cultural schizophrenia, that terror of always being "five minutes out of steerage." The German Jews created a fabulous design for themselves, but New York was never their city. Their desire was to blend, to assimilate, to reproduce their own version of an American aristocracy. They had culture, these Jewish WASPs. They didn't turn their backs on the Russian and Polish Jews; they considered them at least partial brethren and formed societies to "uplift" them and relieve despair, but there was always a rivalry between them. Uptown and downtown. Culture and the wild beards. The wild beards won.

If New York was once an Irish town, it became Jewish and Italian during the first half of this century. The Irish watched their lines of support disappear. They held on to their political machine as long as they could, but even that was taken from them. They just couldn't fight off the rampant energy of Russian Jews. Those wild beards coupled themselves with the Sicilians in a curious way. I'm not talking about Murder, Inc. That's another story. The Italians preserved their sense of a village, forging neighborhoods in Manhattan, Brooklyn, Staten Island, the Bronx, and Queens, neighborhoods that policed themselves with their own families of crime. They wouldn't give up their Sicilian ways, a slow, delicious life, where you could linger over a cup of bitter coffee with a bead of milk on top, while the Jews swarmed around them, going off to college like Yankee Doodle, building vast schemes or sinking into despair, characters out of their own Russian novel.

The Russian Jews were like Krazy Kat, who stands longingly in some eternal present while the landscape keeps shifting around him and he looks for his "dah-link," Ignatz Mouse. George Herriman's "Krazy Kat" is probably the most perverse presentation of the immigrant in any art form. It continues to plague my head forty years after the Kat disappeared (Herriman died in 1944). Krazy was a mysterious creature, male *and* female, a city Kat who could never quite assimilate. He lived in a universe that was near anarchy. The Kat is mortally in love with Ignatz Mouse, who hates his guts. Ignatz's whole constitution is absorbed in the idea of braining the Kat with a brick. The Kat doesn't run. He "waits every moment like a bride for the expected ecstasy, the blow always new and always the same," according to Robert Warshow in *The Immediate Experience*. That Irisher, Offissa Pupp, feels sorry for the Kat and protects him as much as he can. He's eloquent on the subject of Krazy Kat. The Kat's life is "warped with fancy, woofed with dreams."

Woofed with dreams. That's what the wild beards were all about. Krazy is a constant child: obsessive, adoring, brilliant, dumb. He can never graduate to anything. Only the decor around him can change. Not the

Kat. He's frozen in his love. And Ignatz is like some enchanted dream of America, that underside of the immigrant's own self: irrational, shrewd, unadoring. Ignatz will never love Krazy back. Only bricks can materialize from a dream mouse. Bricks for Krazy's head.

The wild beards didn't need Murder, Inc., when they had Krazy Kat and Krazy's secret pals, the Marx Brothers, who were much deeper into "crime" than Dutch Schultz or Abe Reles. The Marx Brothers weren't restrained by Offissa Pupp and his fanciful English. And they wouldn't have been amused by Ignatz Mouse. Harpo and Groucho distrusted everything: governments, children, themselves. They tore the twentieth century down with their antics. They weren't actual greenhorns, but they grew out of the cunning and hysteria of immigrant New York.

The wild beards didn't invent humor, or shouting. It just came natural to them. Low-life immigrants, they discovered that self-mockery was a wonderful defense. It confused your enemies. You could smother them with a laugh. It was David and Goliath all over again, but in the New World, David's slingshot was strung with a howling laugh. Underneath that howl was the terror of isolation, the dread of losing still another country, the fear of that czar who was just around the corner, the czar who would shackle you with his latest subscription service: some dreaded army or an oven.

I'm ethnocentric, I guess. Harlem was once as powerful as the Lower East Side. But until World

War II, blacks were invisible to most whites. Harlem was only one more Chinatown, an exotic place to visit; there were rent parties and the great black clubs, but you couldn't find a black man in Central Park. Harlem itself was born out of Ellis Island, built to encourage an immigrant boom. But it was overbuilt, and when landlords couldn't get their high prices, they rented to blacks, who had little choice of living space and had to pay through the nose. Harlem's boxed-in energy fueled the schizophrenia of this town, the deep split within its own psychic landscape.

New York wasn't a simple tale of two cities. It had always been rich and poor, black and white, ever since the Dutch, who didn't know what to do about their slaves and freed a number of them. But in this century, blacks developed their own institutions that echoed the whites in a sad, bitter way. When the Negro Giants borrowed the Yankee Stadium for their own World Series, it was obvious to whatever white men were around that these Giants could have knocked the pants off most professional white teams. And when Joe Louis came to town, heavyweight champion of the world, he had to room in a Harlem hotel. I'd swear New York is a little less racist than most other cities, but it happened to be the Negro capital of America. With so much ability cooped up, so much psychic wealth, it's no wonder that a craziness abounded in New York, the old lie that the Negro was a "natural child," that he loved to play and would never learn how to spell or keep his money. The blacks, in order to survive, danced to the lie, pretended to be that natural man and woman the whites were looking for. And the whole relationship between blacks and whites became an illness for both parties.

The blacks don't even have Harlem anymore. It's nobody's playland. It's a remembrance, like the Lower East Side. Boulevards have been renamed, but so what? I didn't see much black pride, or anything else, on Adam Clayton Powell Boulevard. It's not even a war zone now. It has its own heroes, like the Reverend Calvin Butts, who's trying to rebuild the politics of Harlem and is also saving lives at the Abyssinian Baptist Church. But Harlem is a ruined village. It's had to give way to Bedford-Stuyvesant, which holds 400,000 of Brooklyn's 723,000 blacks and has been a much more considerable seat of power. Bed-Stuy is being rebuilt, block by block. It has a *mean* political leader, Assemblyman Al Vann, an ex–public school teacher who often tilts with Ed Koch, Ronald Reagan's "friend" in New York.

That's the irony of this metropolis. Our golem mayor appeals to as many Republicans as Democrats. It's the texture of his clay. "I hate radicals," the mayor had told me at lunch. "They have no sense of humor. They're holders of the holy grail. They think of everybody else as shit."

Ah, I shut my mouth and didn't admit to Ed that I was something of a radical, an anarchist with a sense of humor. Krazy Kat. I felt a closeness to Ed Koch. We were an endangered species, the last sons of Ellis Island.

That old mother of an island is now a national monument, and few people will experience that vertigo I felt in the old, crudded registry room, and they really ought to shiver. Shivering is what Ellis is all about.

The main building won't be dolled up in time for the Statue of Liberty's hundredth year. It'll take a while. The roofs will be coppered again. The Guastavino vaults will be scrubbed. The island will have a new canopy, like the one under which the greenhorns traveled from the dock to the station's front door. The station itself will be an elaborate theme park: a palace of immigrant folklore. It will have a computer bank equipped to trace an immigrant's family tree. I'm willing to confront that machine. I might find a Tartar prince somewhere in my blood, or a lot more Polish apple peddlers. I worry about its arrival. With all the remodeling, Ellis will become just another museum.

The ghosts will be gone, and the terror of the place will be put to sleep with slide shows and other attractions. It won't be a haunted castle. The walls and windows will never scream. Ellis will become a slick affair, like the South Street Seaport. I don't want nostalgia. I want the real thing.

Ellis Island crystallized the terror that most immigrants must have felt upon their arrival. First that symbol of America, a copper lady on Bedloe's Island, with her welcoming torch, and then the rude fact: a cattle station disguised as a church, where you were chalked and shunted from bench to bench. Forget the fits of

madness and depression some of the greenhorns suffered. Forget the three thousand suicides.

Suicides can occur on the most enchanted island. But
they do register the pain that must have been endured.
The separation from loved ones and language. The bitter days of steerage. Greenhorns who could afford to
travel first class didn't have to stop at Ellis Island. Ellis is
where the poor landed, speaking no English at all.

Irving Howe can tell us about the tales of assimilation. Fabulous success stories. Immigrants who built
their fortunes on the Lower East Side and moved into
the heartland with their American families. Night-
school wonders who went to Harvard. Their children's
children are now senators and novelists, as American
as Milky Way bars. But what about the madness suffered in almost every family, like some chrysalis that
absorbed the pain surrounding itself, took the pain
inside and fell silent? And the rest of us, who absorbed
pieces of shock and became assimilated bandits, coop-
erative by day but bearing some crazy cultural wound
that shoves in and out of our dreams.

Commandos, possessed by the dark side of the
moon, we don't submit easily to anyone's rule. We're like
Ed Koch, who's more of an anarchist than he thinks.
Growls at everyone, makes people cry. He lives right
inside the city's skin. Golem mayor in a golem town.

Haunch Paunch and Jowl
(1986)

1

THE BONES OF A CITY ARE OFTEN inscribed on a people's back. Particularly in an immigrant town like New York, where whole populations arrived in phantom boats, passed through a brick church while their clothes were chalked and their scalps inspected for lice, and if the country let them in, they toiled to earn their keep, made children, money, and died in the crush to become American. Both the sadness and the vitality of New York come from the same engine: the greenhorn's desire to transform himself into some magical thing, man of the New World. But the New World was as much of a phantom as the old one, because no city could match that vision the greenhorns had of a land where they wouldn't be lonely, where the czar would love them like his very own child. No czar, American or Russian, ever loved a greenhorn.

And it's the frightening distance between the green-horn's invented idea of America and what he finally met that provided the fabric of New York. But it's a fabric with a strange and brutal skin. Because New York is the city that reproduces itself according to the ideals of each generation. It has no continuous line. Everything is possible because its past is only the future turned upside down. New York's history is what happened tomorrow. The Dutch planned it that way. They built a replica of Amsterdam at the foot of Manhattan, a phantom city with windmills and all. And the practical Dutch pretended they were still at home. They weren't *colonists;* They didn't want a New World. They closed their eyes and had their "fabricated motherland." It's no wonder the English took New Amsterdam without a shot. The Dutch were crazy. They thought these gutters and gardens were in some old town. Why should they fight the British for a territory that was as familiar as their own finger? They were Dutch. This had to be Amsterdam. And the English could go to hell.

The Britishers succumbed to that vision. New York remained "new" Amsterdam. The English presence in New York was so illusory because it never took hold. That's why I'd suffered amnesia about the British. They were ruled by Peter Stuyvesant's ghost. And after the redcoats were gone, we still had a Dutch colony, even with the Declaration of Independence. New York was practical and insane. It continued to trade like the Dutch and build on that phantom city. It decided to grow along a grid, ignoring bumps, ditches, and heights, and the particular bend of its rivers. It would be a phantom grid of 2,028 blocks, where anything that was built upon them could be removed at will. So we have the Empire State Building dug into the old cradle of the Waldorf-Astoria. And the Waldorf is shoved onto another grid. We have a Madison Square Garden on Madison Square and then the Garden starts to float, like a gondola on the grid. It reappears uptown, caters to circuses and rodeos, the Rangers and the Knicks, becomes a parking lot, and the Garden is born again over the new Penn Station. It's an ugly glass tank, but who cares? Nothing is sacred except the grid. And the grid doesn't allow for memory and remorse. It's part of a phantom town built onto a Dutch vision of Amsterdam in America, which happens to be called New York.

And so we have a city of perpetual greenhorns. First the Dutch, then those temporary Englishmen, then the Irish, the Germans, the Italians, the Jews, then another wave: Jamaicans, Puerto Ricans, the anti-Castro Cuban middle class, Dominicans, Russian refuseniks, the "black" Cubans out of Mariel harbor, Vietnamese boat people, Koreans, ethnic Chinese from everywhere on the planet, and this country's *internal* immigrants, our Pilgrim slaves, the blacks, who are much older than the Revolution and have a deeper pedigree in America than most of our granddads.

I'd swear on my life that New York became the center of black and Jewish culture partly because of the Dutch. The blacks and the Jews had their own phantom villages, Harlem and the Lower East Side. Slavery was disagreeable to the Dutch. And so was anti-Semitism, in spite of old Peter. And like the Dutch town of New York, Harlem and the Lower East Side sank into their own future, and who can really say what kind of past will emerge?

Narrowed down, New York is nothing but Dutch fathers, the grid, and all the unremembered dead. Sometimes the dead rise up in peculiar ways, and the records they've kept of their lives, their own night songs, begin to haunt us because those songs are often dreams of the city itself. Herman Melville, our greatest fiction writer, had to "die" twice. Once when he stopped publishing stories and novels and became an obscure inspector of the docks. And then when he gave up his own personal ghost in 1891. But Melville was really a twentieth-century writer. It took a time of explosive immigration to rediscover Melville, that man of Dutch and English descent. The nineteenth century, with its absolute faith in the entrepreneur, wouldn't listen to Melville's dark narrative webs. Bartleby the Scrivener haunts our city as no other character in American fiction has ever done. He's like a wicked Dutch ancestor saying no to America's fantastic growth. He's the underside of New York's mercurial energy, city dweller turned into a cocoon.

Bartleby went mad in New York, like the black composer Scott Joplin, who was confined to Manhattan State Hospital after his opera *Treemonisha* failed, and he died there in 1917, brooding over America's loss of interest in ragtime. Joplin was "lost" for fifty years, until his rags were used in *The Sting* (1973), a film that was almost a benign version of Melville's *The Confidence Man,* so much does it depend on thieves tricking other thieves who trick themselves. And in the background are Joplin's syncopations, which are a wonderful counterpoint to all the thievery going on.

There's also Henry Roth, who published *Call It Sleep* in 1934, a Joycean novel of Jewish life in Brownsville at the beginning of the century, and then disappeared. The novel wasn't unnoticed, but there are apocryphal tales about what happened next. Roth was researching a novel on American communism when he was hit over the head near the docks. Roth retreated to the country, where he became a Jewish chicken farmer and a Latin coach at a nearby reform school. He was plucked out of obscurity in 1964, when *Call It Sleep* was reprinted in a paperback edition and reached a million readers. Not even this resurrection could draw him away from his farm. He was still the local chicken slaughterer. But there is nothing in all of Jewish-American literature that compares with Roth's imagination of an immigrant boy in the New World:

> *Standing before the kitchen sink and regarding the bright brass faucets that gleamed so far away, each with a bead of water at its nose, slowly swelling, falling, David again became aware that this world had been created without thought of him.*

And what about those who aren't remembered, who toiled, scratched around, and remained in obscurity: architects, plumbers, bandits, writers, and such, who either fell from grace or never captured a public at all. Samuel Ornitz is a particular example. His novel *Haunch Paunch and Jowl,* published in 1923 as "An Anonymous Autobiography," has more to tell about the relationship between Jews, politics, and crime than any other work of fiction *or* nonfiction. The novel reads like a sociological song. Irving Howe condemns Samuel Ornitz to half a paragraph in *World of Our Fathers* and calls the writing "crude," while he praises *The Rise of David Levinsky,* a much more primitive tale of "success" in the New World, a book written in plodding, clumsy English, full of wistfulness and sentimental meat, with none of Ornitz's raw power. Levinsky is a Jewish-American Everyman, as recognizable as your own grandpa, unless he happens to be an apple peddler.

Ornitz's bibliographer, Gabriel Miller, agrees with Irving Howe. The book feels awkward to him, deficient in form and structure. Miller sees Ornitz's nervous, impressionistic style as no style at all. He's wrong. *Haunch Paunch and Jowl* is a "road" novel about the streets of New York. Miller calls Ornitz's hero, Meyer Hirsch, "one of the vilest characters in American-Jewish literature." Hirsch is lacking in the "Jewish quality" of remorse. Unlike David Levinsky, he has no deep longing for a kinder past. Hirsch *is* monstrous.

He's an authentic child of the New World, a golem without regret.

He's called *ziegelle,* "the little goat," for good reason. A goat was his wet nurse. A goat saved his life. He was born in a ship's manger, three days out of Hamburg, because his dad was running from the czar's military service. His mother had no milk for the baby,

". . . and there was no milk on board." Until a miracle happened. The ship's pet, Hirsch's mother tells Hirsch, "a she-goat with udders plump with milk, escaped from her quarters and came wandering in the steerage . . . and the she-goat suckled my baby and he lived to see the promised land. . . . And so here you are, *mein ziegelle. . . .*"

This goat boy, this child of the New World, is also a child without a country. He's no greenhorn, because he never saw Europe. A goat is his second mother, and his cradle is the sea. He comes to the New World without a single prejudice. Meyer Hirsch has no history. But he does have all the instincts of a goat:

> *A goat manages to get along where any other creature would perish. Stubble, twigs, anything is food and nourishment for him. He is a sidestepper, can walk a narrow ledge or a fence, if need be. He is for himself, unfeeling, and befriends no one. An unlikable, ugly thing with a most unreasonable smell. And I have noticed that a goat is the only thing ridicule can't kill.*

And that's how Meyer Hirsch made his way in the New World. He's the "fourteenth leader" of the Ludlow Street Gang, the last one in line. But Hirsch risks nothing. He's much too clever to steal with his own hands. "I am the cover guy. In other words, I distract the owner and screen the thief." Hirsch gives nothing and always gets. Yet he's pulled into the romance of his gang, "our sweet, lawless, personal, high-colored life," which covers over "the shabbiness, foreignness and crudities of our folks and homes."

Hirsch lives at home with his mother, father, and Uncle Philip, the family philosopher, who despises his bosses, the German-Jewish clothing manufacturers. There isn't enough crockery to go around. Hirsch and Uncle Philip have to eat from the same soup plate.

Philip understands the greenhorn's dilemma. There are no proud grandpas in his line. There's only dust and dead bones. He advises Hirsch: "Meyer, we've got nothing to look back to. It's up to us to be ancestors." Philip starts his own shop and marries into the tribe of German Jews and dies of stomach cancer.

Hirsch sticks to his own kind. He becomes a runner for the local Tammany boss and uses his gang to destroy Republican and Socialist rallies. He goes to law school, builds up an elaborate system of fraud in "that hurly-burly time of New York's nineties," when lawyers, hoodlums, cops, and judges slept in the same "public crib."

Hirsch acquires a mistress, Gretel, a "buxom greenhorn just off the ship," and brings her home as his family's servant. He's crazy about Gretel, but she isn't the kind of girl a pol like him can marry. Hirsch is on the rise. He understands the laws of politics. "Control. Organization. Cash." But he suffers his first defeat when three of his gang members rob and kill a ticket collector on the Second Avenue El and Hirsch can't get them off. They die in the electric chair, but not before one of the gang members reminds Hirsch of "'the potatoes we used to bake in our street bonfires. Do you remember how good they tasted, Meyer; do you remember?' ... And they escorted him through the little green door."

That moment is much more powerful than anything in *The Rise of David Levinsky*. Because Ornitz gives us the rude, dreadful facts without Hirsch's response. Levinsky would have mourned for two paragraphs and evoked half a million potatoes. And we're left with the horror of a little green door.

Meanwhile, Hirsch grows fat. He's the honorable Haunch Paunch and Jowl. He blackmails the Republicans into appointing him a justice of the Supreme Criminal Court. But Gretel has studied his ways. She obliges Hirsch to marry her, and his career is ruined.

By now Hirsch has become "a hulking pachyderm" living on Riverside Drive, Allrightniks Row. He's conquered the New World. Haunch Paunch and Jowl. But all his grasping has gotten him nowhere. He's still that *ziegelle*, sucking on a goat's teat.

Ornitz provides no sentimental choices. Hirsch is nothing more or less than a child caught in the "hurly-burly" of his time. His destiny is to grow fat and never stop feeding. Golem and goat boy, he's now his own ancestor, Haunch Paunch and Jowl.

The novel seemed so accurate and "real" that its publisher, Horace Liveright, decided to present it as the memoir of an actual judge. And Ornitz disappeared from the book. He "introduced" the judge's story and became the anonymous servant of his own fiction. But Liveright couldn't have been so wrong. The book went into seven printings and sold 100,000 copies.

And Ornitz himself? He never had another *Haunch Paunch and Jowl,* no matter what name he used. He wasn't a goat boy, like Meyer Hirsch, and he didn't come off a phantom boat. He was born on the Lower East Side in 1890, the son of Polish immigrants. But he didn't have to share a soup plate with some fictitious uncle. His parents weren't poor. And he wasn't the "fourteenth leader" of any gang. He was an altogether different kind of bandit. A studious little bugger, with glasses on his nose and a writer's bitter heart, like Isaac Babel. He pulled stories out of men and women in the street. *Haunch Paunch and Jowl* wasn't Ornitz's private tale. He was writing about a time that was even more primitive than his own. The book has the urgency of myth. The ghetto itself is born out of goat's milk. Ornitz's greenhorns are like ghosts looking furiously for their own flesh. The ghetto is cluttered with Bartlebys and fat men.

And if Irving Howe sees Ornitz's novel as a marginal text that doesn't admit to the collective assertion of the Jews, I see a different story. There was banditry in that world of sweatshops, and a bitterness that belies the fable of hardworking pioneers on a rough road to success. "Crime," says Irving Howe, "was a source of shame, a sign that much was distraught and some diseased on the East Side; but it was never at the center of Jewish immigrant life."

Crime was also a source of income; it linked politics to the poor. The ghetto was an enormous marketplace, and the potted breast that Hirsch feeds on at the end of *Haunch Paunch and Jowl* is almost like a sacrament; he's devouring the ghetto's blood.

Ornitz understood that the Jewish gangs didn't simply go away as members outgrew their lawlessness. That lawlessness was needed to collect the vote. "The Yiddish gangster is . . . full of business."

Ornitz's own career was typical of a writer with one successful book. He went out to Hollywood, and from 1929 to 1945 he worked on such film classics as *King of the Newsboys, Army Girl, Chinatown Nights, Secrets of the French Police, The Man Who Reclaimed His Head, Portia on Trial,* and *China's Little Devils.* He lived a kind of double life, scratching out mediocre scripts and becoming an anti-fascist organizer.

He was forgotten as a novelist, but notoriety came to him when he was called before the House Committee on Un-American Activities and refused to testify. He spent nine months in prison at Springfield, Missouri, as one of the Hollywood Ten. At Springfield he completed a book that was almost a metaphoric sequel to Meyer Hirsch's life. Called *Bride of the Sabbath*, it reads like a bitter report card about the whole idea of assimilation. It doesn't have the bite of *Haunch Paunch and Jowl*, that mixture of politics and myth, that marvelous sense of Once Upon a Time.

Ornitz died of a cerebral hemorrhage in 1957, an ex-con with a sad tale of America behind him. He couldn't grow fat like Haunch Paunch and Jowl. He didn't have Hirsch's capacity to rush into the darkness and seize a profit for himself. He was only one more deracinated Jew, like the rest of us, "more American than the Americans," without a stinking root, according to Gabriel Miller.

2

I'D LOVE TO REVISIT HIRSCH'S primitive time and look into the romance of Jewish pioneers coming to terms with America. Assimilation broke an awful lot of backs. Jews and Italians were crowded into rookeries that the Irish had just left. In those "hurly-burly" years, the Lower East Side was the meanest part of the world. Nothing compared to the slums of New York. For the uptowners, the "Jewish Street" was an exotic, smelly place, where only animals would live. There was one ferocious preacher, the Reverend Dr. Parkhurst, with his Society for the Prevention of Vice, who blitzed the Allen Street brothels, chasing out whores and all their customers and cadets. But it wasn't until 1894 that the Lexow Committee, appointed by the state senate, "studied" the Lower East Side with Parkhurst's help and exposed all the rich variety of Jewish prostitutes and their helpmates at the Essex Market Court, "lawyers, policemen, and bail bondsmen" who could have been disciples of Meyer Hirsch. The whole East Side was Haunch Paunch and Jowl.

Other committees followed, other investigations. But the whores stuck to Allen Street. There were too many greenhorns around, lonely men with their wives in the Polish Pale. And also customers from uptown, drawn to those red lamps in the windows and the girls who clucked at them from the halls, until Allen Street became the "international" side of the ghetto, a primitive Times Square. It wasn't a street of Talmud Torahs. You could have Russian tea with a lump of dark sugar that cracked in your mouth and go upstairs with an Allen Street girl.

Prostitution was no isolated "disease." It was big business, protected by Tammany pols and the police, in spite of reformers like Parkhurst. But business alone couldn't have created the aura of Allen Street. Allen Street arrived with a profound wish. The greenhorns desired a private place between the downtown sweatshops and communal toilets and the uptown world they feared. "The only thing that interested Jews in Central Park," said the *Daily Forward* in 1905, "was the zoo. They were afraid to venture further into the park lest they get lost." And so the greenhorns discovered that dark and dank strip under the El. Allen Street. Landlords made a fortune renting the bottom floors to whores. There was nothing odd about those "greenie girls," who were as isolated as the men. Some had rebelled against arranged marriages, running to Allen Street from Ellis Island, where they'd met their husbands for the first time. Some of them had been charmed by a cadet. Others preferred lying down with strangers to being sentenced to a sewing machine. And others were industrious girls who saved their money and moved to Prospect Park. There might have been a hundred reasons, but most of the girls were caught between pathology and good sense.

In *Haunch Paunch and Jowl*, Hirsch tells the story of the rabbi, "a thousand years behind the times," who comes to the Grodno Synagogue and learns that the richest members of his congregation own property on Allen Street and "that certain tenants paid ten times as much as ordinary tenants."

The rabbi runs to Allen Street, preaches in the middle of that dark road about "dung upon the Shield of David," and is struck on the head with a blackjack. Hirsch isn't surprised. A rebbe has no business here in the land of red midnight.

But Allen Street wasn't short on piety. The most proper madams wore religious wigs. Allen Street grew into the twentieth century, swollen with greenhorns from Ellis Island. The Jews controlled the gigantic garment industry. Heads were broken during strikes. Polish and Russian Jews became proficient at the art of poisoning horses. It was almost like the Moldavanka district of Odessa that Isaac Babel wrote about. But the Lower East Side didn't have Benya Krik, that romantic hoodlum in raspberry pants, who could fall in love and set fire to a police station in a single instant.

Yes, there was collective assertion on the "Jewish Street." The greenhorns grew less green. They solved the puzzle of Central Park and learned to mingle with uptown Jews. They opened banks on the East Side. Some of them became tycoons. They muttered softly about Jewish crime, as if it existed in a parallel universe, a place they didn't have to touch, although the uptown German Jews weren't quite so blind. The wild beards distressed them, and the German Jews acted out of shame, guilt, or charity, God knows. They began settlement houses and societies to help Jewish prisoners. They grabbed greenhorns coming off the boat, taught them how to dress, exploited them in the shops they owned, and also raised them up. It was all a complicated dance. Love. Hate. Rivalry. It might have continued for years. But something intervened.

In 1908, Theodore Bingham, the police commissioner of New York, wrote in the *North American Review* that half the city's criminals were Jews. Bingham didn't care much for the Italians, either, according to Jenna Weissman Joselit in *Our Gang: Jewish Crime and the New York Jewish Community, 1900–1940*. He called them scoundrels and jailbirds. But he had a particular distaste for the "Russian Hebrews," who, because they were not "physically fit for hard labor," had turned to crime. "They are burglars, firebugs, pickpockets and highway robbers—when they have the courage . . ."

Suddenly the German Jews and those wild beards downtown weren't rivals anymore. They had a common enemy, Theodore Bingham. Uptown and downtown leaders sat in the same room and formed the Kehillah, a watchdog agency that could unite *all* Jews and become their voice among the Gentiles of New York. Bingham apologized, and the Kehillah gathered statistics to prove that the ghetto wasn't a "nursery in crime." But no matter how hard the Kehillah juggled, it couldn't turn Jewish crime into a disappearing act. The Jews were a quarter of the city's population and committed a quarter of the city's crimes. The Kehillah shouldn't have been surprised. The Jews needed gangs, just like the goyim.

The Italians and those "Russian Hebrews" were the city's latest underclass. But the Kehillah wouldn't rest. It started its own police force, the Bureau of Social Morals, and from 1912 to 1922, the Kehillah's detectives roamed the East Side, collecting data on Jewish crime. The Kehillah closed down a hundred brothels, with the help of the city police. Jewish criminals fled from Abe Schoenfeld, the Kehillah's boss of detectives. "Whenever we walked into an underworld dive, they'd say 'Zechs,' which meant 'Stop talking, the Kehillah's here.'" But the Kehillah itself closed down in 1922. And

Schoenfeld's stories began to sound like romantic fiction. Jews were still a quarter of the criminal class.

It was the restrictive immigration laws of the 1920s that weakened the "phenomenon" of Jewish street crime. The nativists had finally won. The National Origins Act of 1924 put an absolute quota on the number of Italians, Slavs, and Jews that could enter the United States: it adhered to the census of 1890, before the "new wave" began, and stopped the flow of immigrants from Eastern and Southern Europe.

But America lost as much as the greenhorns did because the explosion of immigrants at the start of the twentieth century had vitalized America, turned it into a culture of cities. The cities had existed long before the greenhorns arrived; but they were never quite the same after 1900. The greenhorns transformed Chicago, Cleveland, Philadelphia, Boston, Pittsburgh, Baltimore, San Francisco, New York, and Detroit. Suddenly they were "port" cities again, frontier towns, with upheavals of entire populations, bringing creativity and crime.

Crime didn't end with the National Origins Act. But America closed in upon itself, sat in isolation until World War II. It's almost as if the Jazz Age began with the winding down of Ellis Island. America had gone to war in 1917, soaked up Europe's culture and "sin," and then cut Europe out of its vocabulary. The flappers were native American girls. Without the push of new immigrants, the ghetto shrank, and the greenhorns imitated Yankee Doodle. I have pictures of my mom and dad wearing strange American clothes of the 1920s. They look like mannequins, dolls in the service of America. My dad couldn't whistle a word of English, but he looked like John Barrymore's brother.

3

JEWISH DELINQUENCY WAS DOWN. Allen was just another dark street under the El. Ghetto gangsters, like "Dopey Benny" Fein, were gone. The few skinny whores that couldn't find a husband fled uptown. Joselit speaks of the "embourgeoisment of New York Jewry" between the wars. That's a wonderful word, *embourgeoisment*. Like a diorama of Balzac's *La Comédie humaine,* the movement of nogoodniks into the great society. "Somehow," she says, "a Jewish prostitute or a Jewish pimp did not fit in with the happily bourgeois mothers pushing their baby carriages on Ocean Parkway or with the dapper lawyers and garment manufacturers breaking bread at Garfield's, the 'cafeteria of refinement.'"

There were plenty of thugs at Garfield's, between the lawyers and the garment manufacturers. In fact, the thugs looked more dapper than the lawyers themselves. Crime moved out of the ghetto, as the ghetto broke— and even while the ghetto was still that crazy flower of sewing machines, prayer shawls, and a whore's red lamp. Think of Arnold Rothstein, who was mythologized in *The Great Gatsby* as Meyer Wolfsheim, the man who fixed the World Series of 1919. For Scott Fitzgerald, he was a "small, flatnosed Jew" with a large head and "two fine growths of hair which luxuriated in either nostril." Wolfsheim speaks of Jay Gatsby as an "Oggsford man" and asks Nick Carraway if he's looking "for a business gonnegtion." No matter how we chip at the legend, Arnold Rothstein will always be Meyer Wolfsheim. That's the power of Fitzgerald's novel.

Wolfsheim talks like a greenhorn. But Rothstein was born in Manhattan in 1882, the son of a prosperous cotton-goods merchant from Bessarabia, an Orthodox Jew known as "Abe the Just." Rothstein's emergence as the czar of crime is something of a mystery. There's so much fiction surrounding A.R. that not even Meyer Wolfsheim's nostrils can contain all of him. Like Gatsby, he was a man who invented himself. And like Gatsby, he was also shy. While others talked and cursed, "he clicked his teeth and uttered at most a monosyllable."

But A.R. could also curse, and this Bessarabian prince from Manhattan's Upper West Side, with his silken touch, always carried a gun. He had a beautiful blond mistress and a beautiful blond wife. And he died just as mysteriously as he lived. Shot in the groin by a fellow gambler, he was found "crumpled against the wall" at the servants' entrance of the Park Central Hotel and was rushed to the Polyclinic Hospital, where he died without disclosing who his murderer was, writes Donald Henderson Clarke.

A.R. was a notorious "chiseler," and he might have been killed on account of a gambling debt. But if one can believe an old Broadway legend, the *A* and the *R* of the Park Central sign wouldn't light up on the day Rothstein died. Even if it sounds like a bit of Runyon talk, the whole Times Square colony mourned its money lending czar, with or without two dead letters on an electric signboard.

Just "another Jewish boy who had made good," says Irving Howe. After all, A.R. was buried as an Orthodox Jew, "in accordance with the American requirement that, no matter how brutal their lives, gangsters retain a tie of sentiment with the faith of their fathers." Thus the story of A.R. is glamorized to fit the Jewish tradition and Howe's own song of the prodigal son's return to orthodoxy. But Howe neglects to tell us that A.R. had nothing to do with the way he was buried. His father, Abe the Just, demanded a religious funeral for his son.

"Arnold was an anomaly in the history of crime," says Sidney Zion, publisher, reporter, and expert on nogoodniks. The gangsters before and after Rothstein had all been gunmen. You couldn't earn your reputation without a kill. "Meyer [Lansky] was a major-league gunman. If you killed people, they got afraid of you. Arnold was the only guy who didn't kill people."

But how did the son of Abe the Just grow into such a dark prince? He didn't walk out of some cold-water flat and sniff the air of Allen Street. He wasn't Haunch Paunch and Jowl. He was a rich kid from the Jewish West Side. Rothstein was drawn to the ghetto. He disappeared from school and hung around the Jewish faro dens. The poor little rich kid didn't have much of a future until he fell under the influence of Big Tim Sullivan, Tammany's boss on the Lower East Side. "My smart Jew boy," Sullivan called him.

A.R. was jealous of his brother Harry. Thought his parents "loved Harry more." Harry died of pneumonia at twenty, and A.R. spent his life believing he'd "wished his brother's death." Was that brooding look his way of mourning Harry? But he didn't have Wolfsheim's tiny eyes. His eyes were big and brown, his hair was dark, and he had "white, womanish hands," according to Clarke. He was five-seven and looked more like J. D. Salinger than Meyer Wolfsheim. But he wasn't quite so fragile as Salinger's Seymour Glass. A.R. had a "pantherish quickness," or he never would have survived as long as he did.

Through Big Tim Sullivan, he made "gonnegtions" with judges, lawyers, and the police, who began to borrow money from Rothstein. Money was a special kind of liquid in A.R.'s hands. He didn't accumulate it, like other bandits. He spread his money around. A.R. began one of the first laundering operations. Stuffed gambling money into real estate. He was the only bandit who could borrow from the banks. He was the "Wolf," the "Wizard," the "Brain."

His skills weren't really removed from those his father had. He organized like any cotton-goods man. He was the wholesaler of crime. A.R. financed different gangs. He was also a mediator; his word was enough to end a war. "Fitzgerald made him look like a bum," Zion says, wounded by *The Great Gatsby*, "... eating with his hands and all that bullshit. Arnold was a class act. He taught Luciano how to eat."

That shy little man changed the course of American crime. The gang became a business unit under A.R. The Italians probably benefited more from Rothstein than the Jews ever did—wilder, woolier men, like Waxy Gordon and Dutch Schultz. Luciano and Frank Costello were Rothstein's ablest pupils. Costello would inherit A.R.'s role as exclusive banker to the underworld. Costello danced between judges and Tammany pols, the way Rothstein had done. He dressed liked Rothstein, looked like Rothstein, but he didn't have Rothstein's quiet flair. He couldn't sit at Lindy's and nibble cheesecake with Eddie Cantor. He'd never go to a bankers' ball. He wasn't the man Runyon would have written about.

So much of A.R.'s ambience depended on the *idea* of Broadway. Without Times Square, Rothstein would have been an uncelebrated gambler sitting in the shadows. A czar had to be noticed, and Rothstein was seen every night at Lindy's or the Colony Restaurant. He had dinner with his mistress Inez a few hours before he was shot, according to Clarke. "Arnold was very gay—his normal, natural self. ... We spoke of many subjects, but mostly of love; and he said that he hoped soon to be free to marry me. He said everything would be mine—his property and the money—but I cared only for him."

He was at Lindy's when he received the phone call that took him to the Park Central and his death.

Rothstein's own mysterious life helps clarify the significance of Times Square in the psyche of New York. Rothstein was the Wolf, that rootless, remade man who needed the lights of an anonymous lair. Runyon didn't invent the Brain. He could only embroider what he saw. Rothstein never clung to the Lower East Side. He'd been "schooled" in the ghetto, but the Wolf wandered from the faro dens to Times Square, a "free-fire zone" for horse players, hoods, vaudevillians, and whores who wanted to escape their own particular ghetto. In the 1920s, Times Square began to take on something of a Jewish tone. Yiddish became the official argot, not because Times Square was flooded with greenhorns, but because to all the rootless souls, like A.R. himself, Yiddish represented the language of crime.

It wasn't poetry, of course. It was street Yiddish, that special patter of tradesmen and thieves, with its own metaphysics: a bending of the body, a wink, and a mixture of ghetto English and God knows what. Bookies and other sportsmen used it to baffle Irish cops. Comedians played with it in the variety houses and spoke it among themselves, to show the rubes that Times Square had a mother tongue.

Why shouldn't that tongue have been Yiddish? The garment center was only a few blocks away, and most of the bosses were Yids: tight, eccentric men who had their own little court at Lindy's, right next to the creatures of show business. Jolson, Cantor, Fanny Brice, and her gambler husband, "Nicky" Arnstein, lived at Broadway hotels. The humor, the style, the frantic energy of Broadway was Jewish. Times Square was almost like the Lower East Side's secular shadow, a Yankee Second Avenue without melameds and Jewish mothers beckoning their sons to attend City College and their daughters to marry a doctor.

And presiding over this wolf's lair until the end of 1928 was a polite gangster, A.R., friend of Fanny Brice and "Roxy" Rothapfel, the movie-palace king. He wasn't like Benya Krik, a boisterous, romantic outlaw in ghetto pants. He was the Jewish Gatsby. The irony of it all is that Fitzgerald had uncovered the wrong Arnold Rothstein. Fitzgerald was a perennial Princeton boy, and Meyer Wolfsheim was Princeton's version of the Broadway Jew, endearing and vulgar. It was Rothstein who could have "picked out the green light at the end of Daisy's dock," Rothstein who "believed in the green light, the orgiastic future that year by year recedes before us." And Fitzgerald never knew it.

4

I'm not Rothstein and I'm not Isaac Babel. I have no Odessa tales, no Moldavankas in Manhattan, or a bestiary of Jewish gunmen, labor racketeers. Lepke and Gurrah and all that crowd. Or, as one of Lepke's hitmen lamented to Sidney Zion, "We were bigger than the Italians. You think we took orders from the guineas? Meyer [Lansky] sold off the empire. We lost our farm teams."

That's the American way—images of baseball reaching into crime. And I'm not about to start a war between the Italians and the Jews. How can I say whose farm teams were the best? But the Italians had one distinct advantage. They didn't bother their heads with any maddening drive into the middle class. The Jews went to City College and the Italians stayed at home.

The Italians haven't produced ghost cities like Brownsville and the East Bronx. They didn't fabulate a Grand Concourse for themselves and then disappear to the ends of the earth, running from phantom tribes of blacks. The Italians weren't like those Yiddish Ponce de Leóns, with Miami Beach in their blood. But they have their own peculiar mindscape: they'd gone through Ellis Island like goat boys, clinging to the Sicilian rocks. Those "black" Italians concocted hilly towns in the flatlands of New York. That was their genius and mad strength. Nothing existed outside the family and the village.

It was perfectly natural that families would organize into tribal units, police themselves, and turn to crime. They were ghetto brats, after all. They exploited strangers and protected themselves. And the stronger tribes began to exploit the weakest ones. They owned entire blocks, created fiefdoms for themselves. Having been the lowest order of a feudal system, little better than donkeys, they decided to become lords. But their old-fashioned ways would have doomed them in the New World. They couldn't compete with the rough Irish gangs, who had Irish judges and Irish cops behind them. They could barely enter the Irish church. There were no Italian cardinals in New York. The Irish had completely shut them out.

And so the Italians turned to their fellow green-horns, the Yids, who were also goat boys and dreamers, with their shtetls on both sides of Grand Street, and their medieval-eyed look that was as familiar as the water of Naples. They fought the Irish hoods, became gunmen in the same gangs. And the best of them worked for Arnold Rothstein, the Wolf of Broadway.

But the young Italian lords were left without a financial wizard after A.R. was shot in the groin, and they began to organize along his lines. They weren't only hit men. A.R. had taught them the business of crime. They had lawyers and accountants, just like A.R., and made peace with the judges and the cops. They discovered the persuasion of money outside their own little shtetls. They could buy a judge or finance Tammany Hall. Tammany might never have survived the lean years of La Guardia without Italian (and Jewish) gang money. Lepke *and* Costello contributed to the Wigwam. But Costello was the better accountant. Lepke was linked to Murder, Inc., and died in the electric chair after surrendering to Walter Winchell. And Bill O'Dwyer, who, as Brooklyn's district attorney, helped bring Lepke down, visited with Frank Costello, the don of Tammany Hall, before becoming mayor of New York.

The Italian bandits persevered because they held to their home base. The Jews couldn't sit still. They found their own suburbs. They went to Havana and opened Las Vegas, until the dons took their little empires away. Meyer Lansky was furious at the portrait of himself in *Godfather II,* where Al Pacino, playing Michael Corleone, has him killed. Sidney Zion, who met Lansky in Israel, says, "Meyer went crazy . . . he couldn't stand the humiliation of a Jew being shot by a dago. It really, really pissed him off."

But the dons still won. Lansky is dead, and five families rule New York: Gambino, Colombo, Genovese, Luchese, and Bonnano. Like sweet noises out of an opera book. Their main kingdom isn't Mulberry Street anymore. The dons crossed the bridge years ago, before the Dodgers drifted to L.A. They have their own Little Italy at Bath Beach, which is isolated from tribes of tourists and is run like a Sicilian town of the New World, with capos, soldiers, and geeps, who are at the bottom of the mob's pole. The geeps are not "made men," official soldiers of the five families. The dons import them from Sicily.

The geeps are the newest generation of goat boys, with all the wildness of the Sicilian rocks. They act as "mules" (dope smugglers) and hit men. They're impossible to trace because they have no criminal records. They're zips. They marry here, in the Brooklyn veld, but the dons don't like them to live in Bath Beach (too many goat boys can spoil a neighborhood). The geeps have to find their culture among the Latinos of north Brooklyn. Their home is on Knickerbocker Avenue, a tiny Italian enclave near the Queens border. But as the geeps become simple soldiers in a crime family, their status improves. And the dons allow them to move closer and closer to Bath Beach, until they're on Cropsey Avenue and they've lost that greenhorn look.

But sometimes this feudal hierarchy of dons surrounded by soldiers and geeps falls down. Tommy Eboli, the former head of the Genovese family, was murdered by his own troops because Tommy didn't pay enough attention to their needs. Zips had been brought down from Canada to do the job. They shot him in the face as he was leaving his girlfriend's house. The family named a new acting head, Frank Tieri, known as "Funzi," or the "Frenchman," because he had a thick, froggy voice. Funzi took better care of his troops, and he died a natural death.

That much I knew, but it was still hard for a kid from the Bronx to travel around Bath Beach with a notebook in his hand. The Gambinos, with their two thousand soldiers, wouldn't have liked a novelist in their midst. And so I asked my brother to take me on a tour of Bath Beach. He'd worked the old precinct at the corner of Bath Avenue and Bay 22nd, which looked like a nineteenth-century bank with a castled roof. It was a good place to start a pilgrimage.

I saw the limousine services, the auto-repair shops, around which a Caddy parked in the street wouldn't last twenty minutes. I saw the young geeps standing outside the Caffe Paradiso, dressed in silk shirts, their eyes like dark white teeth. They might live on Knickerbocker Avenue, but the Paradiso was theirs that night.

I had dinner with my brother Harvey at the Villa Borghese on Bath Avenue, the heart of Italian country. The geeps at the other tables looked at us. Their silk shirts seemed to bloom in the dark of the Borghese. They clicked their teeth and talked in a lower voice. It was Harvey they were worried about. I was much too skinny to have the proper stink of a detective. They must have thought I was Harvey's buff, a mook in Trotsky glasses.

The owner arrived at our table, asked how Harvey was, and returned to the kitchen. "I just gave him a heart attack," Harvey said. But there wasn't much of a crisis at the Villa Borghese. The geeps drank their minestrone, and Harvey and I tore at Italian bread. There was so much eyeballing between the tables, it began to feel like a company of friends.

I talked to Harvey about our dad. But he wouldn't remember the crazy fights at home, the broom my father had thrown at him in a rage, and Harvey's swollen eye.

"Ah, I don't dwell on it," he said.

He told me about Vinnie the Mook, the ancient retarded boy of Bath Beach, who wore a phony police badge and could go into any restaurant and eat for free.

Who cares how the economy went? It was a village. Even the mob had an obligation to a mook.

But I didn't meet Vinnie, and I don't think the geeps would have sat for an interview. Yes, I'd become a scholar of the Maf. I knew which tribes carted garbage and which tribes wouldn't. But I kept searching for some clue into the private machinery of the dons. I didn't want books and magazine articles, confessions of a Mafia princess. I wanted the real thing, a disgraced button man who would talk to me. And then I found my man. That is, my brother found him for me. A former rat in the Federal Witness Protection Program. He was living out on Long Island under an assumed name. He wasn't interested in money. He was a police buff. He liked to brag about his exploits, my brother said. But Harvey had never met the guy. We had to use a go-between. The stoolie was playing hide-and-seek. But he had stories about the Maf. Guaranteed. All we had to do was open him up, encourage the stoolie, get him to sing.

The stoolie was as temperamental as any diva. Three months went by and he still wasn't singing. He'd say yes, no, and yes again. Then my brother called me. "Kid, the meet is on." Took the subway out to Coney Island and got into my brother's car. We didn't have to hurry. The go-between was late. We went in *his* car to another village, where we finally met our man, the federal informant. He had a tattoo on his arm, and I wondered if he was like the Yakusa, those Jap button men who colored their bodies according to the horrors of their particular clan.

I'll call him "Moey" because I'd rather not get him killed. He lived in a ranch house with a woman who could have been his wife. She offered me a Pepsi-Cola. And I began to think less and less of this Yakusa and his tattoo. What the hell were colored pinpricks on an arm? The guy had never been a button man. He didn't have the right kind of fatness. There was something Talmudic about him. He was soft in the middle, like a scholar. He had horn-rimmed glasses and an owl's eye. He'd never worked for the dons a day in his life. Wasn't even Italian.

Thought I could smell the Bronx on him. I wasn't so wrong. He was a Jew from Bensonhurst, not the kind of Jew Irving Howe would write about. Moey was a confidence man, a carryover from an earlier, rougher time. And then I understood why he seemed so familiar. It had nothing to do with memories of Brooklyn or the Bronx. This was my old friend Meyer Hirsch, Haunch Paunch and Jowl, hurled into another time and place. He wasn't a judge eating potted breast on Allrightniks Row. He was an anonymous man with a new identity card, some federal prosecutor's sweet little boy, a former pet of the United States.

But Meyer-Moe didn't behave like a pet. He was indignant about the government's protection plan, which was supposed to shield an informant after he testified, give him money, and a "new fucking life." Never worked out that way for Moe, who was one of the first witnesses in the plan. "They said, 'We'll give you twenty-nine hundred a month.' They gave me balls

... screwed up on my Social Security. I could have gotten better papers on my own."

He bitched and bitched, but my brother had been right about him. Moe was a buff. He'd come out of the cradle with his own grift. "The witness program sucks." But he loved being a confidence man for the FBI. "The prosecutors told me they didn't care what I do as long as I don't rob banks or kill people. I was a one-man strike force."

And how did it all begin for Moe? He'd gone into the automobile business with some mook. "I was in business with the guy for thirty days ... borrowed money from my mother, and thirty days later I was busted in five different counties, like Al Capone." It wasn't Moey's fault that the cars he was trading were hot. His partner had set him up. "I knew the guy. He just burned me. Not a dime in the bank and I got busted. He nailed my ass to the wall."

And that's when the federal prosecutors took to Moe and turned him around. He ran with the FBI, the Secret Service, and the special task force on narcotics. Moe was involved in every sort of sting operation. "I passed off a million dollars in counterfeit money. I pulled down a hundred-million-dollar jewel case." It was hit and run for Meyer-Moe. "I went from agency to agency. . . . I did a lot of things on my own. I gave D. [one of the prosecutors] a shit hemorrhage."

Moe moved about America, working his stings. Melville would have adored such a confidence man.

Drugs were Moe's specialty. "I did so much in drugs, never less than five kilos. When people begged me for a kilo, I said you can get that from the niggers on the street."

Moe crisscrossed the country like some terrible, teasing Lolita with a butterfly net. He has an active memory about all the specimens he trapped: 448 convictions, 640 arrests. "I buy weight," he said to a dealer in Miami known as the "Black Jew." He'd set himself up in Miami Beach as a merchant prince, with his own prostitutes and federal agents performing as his bodyguards. Moe even had a swimming pool. It was like a story out of the *Arabian Nights*, with Moe as Scheherazade *and* the fat king who wasn't allowed to doze. And we were Scheherazade's witnesses. The Black Jew offered to sell three kilos. Moey wouldn't bite. "I need more volume," he said, offering the dealer a prostitute at the pool. The dealer took the prostitute, but he had to beg for time. They would finish the "buy" on the phone.

"Don't talk dope on the telephone, talk about shoes, black shoes," Moey said. The dealer called. He had six black shoes to sell. But he had to leave Miami to get them.

The dealer returned, got off the plane with "a gorgeous babe and six black shoes," and Moey's bodyguards arrested him on the spot. That was the end of the Black Jew of Miami.

"Did you get any of the action?" the go-between asked.

"Balls," Moe said. "I was supposed to get fifteen thousand dollars in that hundred-million jewel sting. I got five. And the U.S. marshals are still holding the jewels."

But Moe's story wasn't about money or the excitement of a sting. Moe didn't see himself as a stoolie. "I wasn't a rat. A rat spills on his friends." He was a government whirlwind, Moe the attack ship, Batman let out of his cave and lent to the FBI. But it was more than that. He'd lived a kind of schizoid life, doing scams in the morning and attending his son's bar mitzvah in the afternoon. He was like a Hollywood producer orchestrating his own skits on the government's Monopoly board. Moe had all that money to play with and agents to move around. "I did it as a challenge," he said. But there was a madness to Moe. His stings had little to do with the ordered world of the FBI. He was Haunch Paunch and Jowl, the con man who'd finally conned himself. He'd become a fantasist, a make-believe Moe, undercover cop without a badge, the ultimate grifter.

But he grew tired of the fantasy and the federal marshals who were supposed to protect his life. This was the very same marshal service that had policed the West. According to Moe, the marshals "got a few people killed because of their ignorance." Marshals shouldn't have been allowed to handle a prize witness like Moe. "They were giving me six hundred dollars a month . . . and no job."

Moe gave up the glory. "I don't want to work with marshals," he told the feds. "Give me some money, let me get away, and I'll take care of myself."

He went back to selling cars, and I wasn't any closer to the dons of Bath Beach. But the go-between saw my distress and began pumping Moe. "Did you work any stings against the mob?"

"No," he said. "But Funzi saved my ass."

Ah, the Frenchman. We were back in Genovese country.

"Funzi buys a car from me," Moe said, talking about one of his incarnations as an auto dealer. "I ask him, 'how do you want it registered?' Funzi sees an exit sign and says, 'Register it as Joe Exit.'"

But Moe was chased out of that dealership and bought a bar on Nostrand Avenue. A pair of geeps tried to shake him down. They were minor soldiers of a minor don, but they wanted a little piece of the bar for themselves.

"You can't have it," Moe said. "I'm a connected man."

"Who's your rabbi?"

"I'm not allowed to tell."

The geeps sneered at Moe, examined his stock of whiskey, and warned him they'd be back that night at nine. Moe got Funzi on the phone. "Don't worry," the Frenchman said. "I'll call at nine-fifteen." The geeps returned and Moe waltzed with them until the phone rang.

"That's my rabbi," Moe said, and the geeps picked up the phone, listened for half a minute, "had a shit hemorrhage, and walked out the door."

Moe wanted his life turned into a television series,

and he needed a novelist. But I wasn't the right person to chronicle his tales with the FBI. I couldn't make him glamorous enough. He was Haunch Paunch and Jowl, corpulent con man. More Zero Mostel than Robert Redford, and Zero wasn't even alive.

We left the stoolie in his ranch house.

"He's had a charmed life," I said.

The go-between agreed. "Moe couldn't have survived today with all those Colombian madmen. He's a fucking dinosaur. And he was careful. He never messed with the Chin," meaning Genovese chieftain Vincent Gigante. "The Chin would have eaten him alive."

We drove back to my brother's car, and I took the local to New York. I thought of the television series I'd never write about Moe. Tales of a federal informant. With Scott Joplin in the background, a bit of sting music. And some blue-eyed discovery to play Moe as a much sleeker man. Who cares? I'd still call it *Haunch Paunch and Jowl.*

Isaac Babel
(2004)

1

IT'S THE ONE BOOK I HAVE TWO COPIES OF. They sit side by side. *The Collected Stories of Isaac Babel* (circa 1960), with Milton Glaser's cover of three Cossacks on horseback wiggling against a white background like quarks or some other magic material suddenly visible to the eye. Glaser has caught both the ferocity and the fragile charm of Babel, whose language seems to slice at us while his characters float across our field of vision. Babel is dangerous; he disturbs our dreams. He's cruel *and* tender, like some kind of crazy witch. Each of his best stories—"The King" or "Di Grasso" or "Guy de Maupassant"—is like a land mine and a lesson in writing; it explodes page after page with a wonder that's so hard to pin down. The structure of the stories is a very strange glass: we learn from Babel but cannot copy him.

I've lived with him nearly all my adult life. I discovered Babel *after* I'd written a novel and read Nabokov, Faulkner, Hemingway, James Joyce, Scott Fitzgerald,

121

Jane Austen, Saul Bellow, and Grace Paley. I was sitting with my editor in an Italian restaurant filled with mafiosi. He himself was a novelist, and every other editor in New York feared him, because he was a pirate who ransacked publishers' lists and stole authors at will. He didn't have to steal me. I was his single discovery, his one dark horse. And for a short period, just before my first novel was published, while he bickered with book clubs and lined up blurbs that he himself would write and then ask one of his stolen authors to sign, I remember having lunch with him every day of the week.

He happened to compose one of the blurbs while we were finishing our hazelnut cake (reserved for him and me) and coffee with lemon peel. "Incomparable," he scribbled on the tablecloth. "Stupendous." I was embarrassed at his flamboyance, and the liberties he took with the restaurant and its tablecloths. "Babel is the one and only writer who comes to mind."

"Couldn't you be a little less exotic? Who's this Babel?"

He revealed his disappointment by crushing the lemon peel and canceling all our other lunches. He wouldn't talk to me (or write another blurb) until I'd read Isaac Babel. I was whisked into another dimension, where everything to do with my book stood still. I had a book jacket with my name on it but with the title missing. I had a photograph of me with half a face. I had the proofs of every fifth chapter. I found Babel's stories in a bookshop, but I resisted reading him until I fell upon "The King" and its perverse outlaw in orange pants who reigned over Odessa and disposed of his enemies by firing bullets into the air. He was called Benya Krik, and he was so recognizable that I suffered through palpitations of pleasure and pain.

Benya's native territory was a Jewish slum, the Moldavanka, home of gangsters and grocers and mythical draymen, a ghetto of dark streets that seemed outside ordinary time, suspended in the reader's own imagination. I'd met this Benya before, many times, in *my* Moldavanka, the East Bronx, where he was always defiant in his orange pants. He wasn't a drayman. His shoulders weren't broad, but he walked with his own marvelous ballet, giving out candy to all the kids. His nails might be dirty, his shoes unshined, but he was still a gallant. He didn't seek wealth, but a kind of feudalism, a fief that belonged to him and him alone. The grocers gave him food, and no one would dare steal a solitary fig from them. We never took our problems to the police—they were from another planet, aliens who didn't bother to understand our sins. The important thing was that our Benya with the dirty fingernails had no fear of them. He ruled even if he never got rich. He was the lord of empty space, prince of those without a language other than the glaring musicality of his orange pants. . . .

I read on and on. I found myself going back to the same stories—as if the narratives were musical compositions that one could never tire of. Repetition increased their value. Babel was involving me in merciless fairy tales that evoked the first books I'd ever read. With each dip into Babel I discovered and rediscovered reading itself.

I bought another copy, savored it, put it on my shelf. I wouldn't travel anywhere with my two Babels. I didn't want the binding to break. I knew nothing about him until I read the introduction beneath Milton Glaser's cover of the three wiggling Cossacks. Babel died in a concentration camp in 1939 or 1940, according to Lionel Trilling (he was murdered in the cellars of the Lubyanka; his executioner didn't fire into the air, like Benya Krik). "It has been said that he was arrested when Yagoda was purged, because he was having a love-affair with Yagoda's sister." I put a check near that sentence; the name Yagoda seemed poetic and sinister at the same time. And I couldn't stop thinking about Yagoda's sister. Yagoda himself was chief of the Cheka (Stalin's secret police). And I couldn't have known it then (few people did), but Trilling had the wrong police chief and the wrong relative. Babel had had an affair with Evgenia Yezhova, wife of Nikolai Yezhov, the Cheka chief who came after Yagoda. Yezhov was one of the great killers of the twentieth century, next to Stalin. And Evgenia and Babel died because of Yezhov, a little man with a limp. But I only learned that years after my original romance with Babel. . . .

My pirate of a publisher never took me back into the fold. He disclaimed me as his one dark horse. My novel appeared, but only with a minor hiccup from a book club, and no blurbs. I had my compensation: Babel. In 1937, at the height of Stalin's terror machine, with Yezhov in power, Babel was obliged to give an interview before the Union of Soviet Writers. The questions asked of him were absurd. I offer one in particular: Why was Babel interested in the *exceptional?*—as if this were a crime. It was a crime under Stalin. But without the *exceptional*, we would have no Benya Krik, no stories about Babel's own ride with the Red Cavalry, no sense of a poetic, troubled language that reverberates in every direction, bathes us in the blood of verbs and nouns.

Babel had to give an answer. It was as absurd as the question, but with a little tongue of truth. Tolstoy, he said, "was able to describe what happened to him minute by minute, he remembered it all, whereas I, evidently, only have it in me to describe the most interesting five minutes I've experienced in twenty-four hours. Hence the short-story form" (*You Must Know Everything*).

And I carry Babel's "five minutes" in my head wherever I go. It has nothing to do with Tolstoy, with *War and Peace* versus *Red Cavalry*, or with large canvases versus small. Babel's "five minutes" were about creating volcanoes with each sentence, about conjunctions on the page that are closer to jazz riffs than to any writer (including Tolstoy), about a strange autobiographical journey in which Babel mingles with killers and rabbis, Cossacks and painters of icons, the beautiful wife of a Petersburg banker whose only dream is to translate Maupassant, philosophers with their eyes plucked out, Marxists with bullets wrapped in phylacteries; he takes us where we've never been and where we could never go—into the incredible lost land of art that Milton Glaser captures with his three cavaliers. Babel lived inside language, lived inside myth, settled there, a Headless Man whose single desire was to turn his existence into a wondrous tale.

2

In July 2003, I went on a pilgrimage to Washington, D.C., to interview Nathalie Babel. I didn't know what to expect when I knocked on Nathalie's door. Should I call her "Natasha," the name under which Babel had known his little Russian daughter, who happened to have been born in France? I admired her fierce devotion. She'd become Babel's "editor" in the United States, had gathered his stories and letters . . . like a cunning cadet.

"Being Russian, French, American, and Jewish has meant that wherever I am, part of me could be somewhere else." She could also have been writing about her father, who was always "somewhere else," whether in his own mind or on some crazy gallop from place to place, or about wanderers like myself who'd traveled from their own "Odessa" on some rocking horse of words.

I felt close to Nathalie. Was she really the child of that Headless Man? When she opened the door, I didn't have any doubt. She looked like Babel, had the wondrous truculence of her father's face, like a little commissar of mind and imagination. I'd been told she was a tough customer. Nathalie herself had said on the phone that she'd scared off another interviewer. He'd come all the way from Montreal and wanted to camp outside her apartment, question her for ten hours at a clip. But his first question was fatal. "Who are the Shapochnikoffs?" he asked. (Shapochnikoff was the married name of Isaac's sister, Maria.) But I had studied the whole Babel tree, including the Shvevels (his mother's family), the Gronfeins (his first wife's family), and the Shapochnikoffs.

I asked Nathalie about her mother, Zhenya Gronfein.

"She's the one who intrigues me," I said, the dark lady from Kiev (with reddish brown hair), who'd been dismissed by Ilya Ehrenburg and others as a bourgeois beauty. The entire Soviet Union, it seems, had condemned her because her father happened to be rich before the Revolution. She'd been written out of Babel's life, expunged. We have Antonina Pirozhkova's testimony, her years with Babel—the pieces of string, Babel's fear of forests (was he still haunted by the Red Cavalry campaigns near the end of his life?)—but we have nothing from the first Mrs. Babel, who was so unlike the second. . . .

Nathalie would grow up without the usual children's stories. She had Isaac Babel. "Mother read the stories to me as a child. She admired them very much." It wasn't only Antonina who recalled Babel's piece of string. Zhenya had told Nathalie about that habit of his. "They were in the Caucasus [it was 1922]. He would work at night, with a piece of string, and every day he would read to her what he was working on."

Zhenya had fond memories of Batum, where she lived with Babel on the side of a mountain and had to hike for miles on unsafe roads in order to reach the nearest market. There were "hard times" on Babel's mountain, yet "they were happy together." An "heiress" from Kiev, "she didn't have the slightest idea of how to cook. But she decided she had to cook." And when she made Babel soup for the first time, "he put his knife into it. The knife stood up in the soup."

Babel worked like a madman on his mountain. And then there was the move to Moscow, when his writing began to unravel. Enter Tamara Kashirina, the Russian Delilah who entangled herself with the weak-eyed Samson of Soviet literature. And Babel scrawled his *Avtobiographiya* that same year: 1924. It begins to make sense why he didn't include his marriage to Zhenya, a daughter of the Jewish bourgeoisie. He'd had his second birth, as a Soviet writer called Kiril Lyutov, the fictitious narrator of *Red Cavalry*, who'd also "lost" a wife. The nom de guerre he used was hardly an accident—*lyuty* in Russian means "wild, ferocious," as if Babel were pretending to be "ferocious" as a Cossack, or as "wild" as language itself, or could borrow his persona from the Revolution, cut off the past with some of the same violence. But the man who rode with the Cossacks wore an invisible skullcap. He had a tribe as compelling as the Cossacks themselves....

Zhenya couldn't forget the string of pearls her father hid from the Bolsheviks. Gronfein "twisted that string of pearls into the electric cord hanging from the ceiling. [And he did it just before the era] of Bolsheviks entering your house and grabbing everything— muzhiks coming in and threatening everybody," after

1917. Her father "died first and quickly." Zhenya had already gone to France, where she had neither friends nor family, and she asked Babel to bring her "certain mementos" of her dead father; Babel found "two small ivory cigarette holders—that's all."

3

I HAD TO TRACE THE PATH of the two ivory pieces. So I'm on a second pilgrimage—to the land of Maupassant, looking for Babel's first address in Paris: Villa Chauvelot. But Villa Chauvelot has disappeared from the map. And so I wander into some labyrinth at the edge of Paris, in the fifteenth arrondissement, right near the *périphérique,* a sinister road that circles Paris like a hangman's knot. Babel's old neighborhood is in a *bidonville* where boulevards float into nothingness. I find the rue Chauvelot, which must have contained its own cul-de-sac, a blind alley with little houses where Babel had lived at number 15, but the whole "Villa" has been swallowed up by a modern housing development with broken balconies at the corner of the street. I reconnoiter on the rue Chauvelot like a Cossack commander, circle around the street to the impasse du Labrador, another cul-de-sac, which butts into the side wall of the housing project. I want to explore a bit, to uncover traces of Babel's blind alley, but a wolf-hound sits deep within the impasse and stares at me with his Siberian eyes, and I'm obliged to retreat....

Babel left for Paris in July 1927 and didn't return until

October of the following year. Was he seeking some sort of reconciliation with Zhenya? A Headless Man capable of multiple lives (with multiple women), he arrived with his mother-in-law, Berta Davidovna, like a Russian Yankee Doodle prepared to conquer Paris. He lived among the "deaf-mutes," as the Soviets called capitalists in the West, for fifteen months, a dangerously long time, even for a writer of Babel's repute, a writer with a wife already in France (since December 1925), and a mother and sister in Belgium. It looked like the intrigue of an exile, someone who was planning to stay among the "deaf-mutes." And indeed, exile must have been on Babel's mind. French was his own first love. Hadn't he announced himself as the new Maupassant? Hadn't he visited Paris in his psyche long before he arrived, crowing to his writer friends about the frilly pink lamp shades of Maupassant's last flat? He was fluent in French. And he was lonely, often desperate, without his mother and sister near him. He would become crazed whenever letters didn't arrive. "Write, write, write" is the chronic complaint in his own letters. "You're knifing me."

What kind of welcome could he have hoped for in France? He'd been living on and off with Tamara [his Moscow mistress], had a "love child" to legitimize their liaison. Yet Zhenya, the little bourgeoise, as Ilya Ehrenburg called her, did welcome him back. She would tremble before he arrived, with anticipation *and* anger probably, over his love affairs (there was more than one Tamara) and the birth of the little boy. Zhenya would have known about the child, no matter how evasive Babel was: Moscow was a land of blabbermouths. And Zhenya kept that secret from Nathalie herself. It was only in 1957, when she was dying in a public ward in Paris, that she opened up to Nathalie.

"I left Russia mostly because of an affair your father was having with an actress, a very beautiful woman. She pursued him relentlessly, and didn't care that he was married. She wanted him and his fame, and had a son by him. Perhaps one day you might meet this man, and you should know he is your half brother and not someone you could fall in love with."

Why did she play Cassandra on her deathbed? Zhenya must have been carrying that same wound for thirty years; the reality of little Mischa (or Emmanuel) disturbed her much more than any mistress. And so she obsessed that Nathalie might fall in love with her half brother, as if she imagined parts for Nathalie and Mischa in some Sophoclean drama. But Nathalie wasn't living in Moscow; there was little chance she would ever meet that anonymous boy. And yet the possibility plagued Zhenya like a little tale of incest. How many times must she have imagined that boy, wished to annihilate him, or steal him from Tamara? And it was into this imbroglio that Babel crept, the infected husband who was already notorious among Russian émigrés as the man who swore he'd served in the Cheka.

We have no diaries or agendas of Babel's day-to-day existence in Paris. We know that he met Feodor

Chaliapin in 1927, and that Chaliapin, the most adored actor-singer of his era, complained to Babel of his own unhappiness and neglect. And Babel felt the same neglect as Chaliapin. He was only a "skeleton" in Paris, one more Soviet writer in a land where writers weren't treated like national treasures or holy men. No one stopped him in the cafés, demanded his autograph. No one talked like Benya Krik. He would hike to Montparnasse from the Villa Chauvelot, sit in the Dôme or La Coupole with his émigré friends, such as Boris Souvarine, a charter member of the French Communist Party until he was kicked out in 1924, and Yuri Annenkov, a celebrated painter and portraitist, and he would grumble to them about his disenchantment with the Revolution, but everybody grumbled. The Cheka could have been sitting with him at La Coupole. Tsarist generals were kidnapped right off the streets of Paris. . . .

Did Babel's jeremiads mean that he intended to elope *permanently* to Paris? In letters to his mother and Maria, he harps about Zhenya's playboy brother, Lyova, who was on the verge of becoming an American millionaire. And Babel had to wait until Lyova's situation became solid. "This is a very important point in planning our future existence." But Lyova's situation would never become solid. He was always about to sign some contract with an American mogul. And Babel waits and waits. "No news from Lyova at all." It seems odd that Babel counted on this phantom brother to deliver him from the bondage of being poor in Paris, like some totem or symbolic wish that would have allowed him to break with the Soviets, be near Maria and his mother, mend his marriage. . . .

Zhenya didn't leave any portraits of Babel in Paris, but his old school chum Lev Nikulin did. Nikulin happened to be in Paris at the same time as Isaac Babel. "On his first visit to Paris, Babel seemed to melt into the background of the city. He soon lost interest in Montparnasse, the Coupole, and the Dôme [Hemingway's hangout], and would often come to see us on the Avenue de Wagram, or rather on the rue Bréa [Nikulin means the rue Brey], where, in the cheap Hôtel Tilsit[t], all kinds of people lived—Russians and various foreigners of no fixed occupation."

Babel kept to his mysterious, mandarin ways. He wouldn't phone in advance. He'd appear at the hotel without warning, capture Nikulin, oblige him to trek across Paris. They stopped in front of a bordello one morning in Montmartre, looked through the windows at the debris inside. Babel wanted to know if the bordello kept its own books. "It would be fascinating to study the entries in the books. They would make a chapter in a good novel," one that Babel himself might have written, with its own stark geometry—mirrors, money, and lace pants. . . .

And then there was Volodya—a Russian taxi driver who also lived at the Tilsitt. "In autumn, in bad weather, he didn't have much business and he'd drive us round the city at half price. We would go along slowly, stopping by the Seine, or in the Latin Quarter, or the ancient little square at the back of the Pantheon." They would observe Paris in the "eerie, phosphorescent glow" of the gaslights. And years later, Babel would recall these "nocturnal trips" and say to Nikulin, "How nice it would be to go for a ride with Volodya again."

His friends in Moscow mistook the Villa Chauvelot for some luxurious mansion in the middle of Paris, but Babel had to shrink within the walls of his cul-de-sac. "I lead a most simple life," he explained to one of these friends. "I write. I can't sit for more than three francs' worth of coffee. I don't have much money. There's nothing to have a good time on. I walk around the streets of Paris and look closely at everything. I avoid old acquaintances and don't look for new ones. I go to bed at eleven and that turns out to be late" (quoted in Patricia Carden, *The Art of Isaac Babel*).

"[I]t is clear that settling down in the West would not have suited Babel," says Lev Nikulin. Babel "could not do without the hectic, helter-skelter life of the country that was dearest to him." But Nikulin himself had returned to Moscow. Souvarine and Annenkov did not, and they could feel the frustration in Babel. "Here [in Paris] a taxi driver has more freedom than the rector of a Soviet university," he said to Annenkov.

Babel was waiting for some deliverer. "I can't sleep nights. I have a terrible cold, my eye is all puffed up and full of matter. All in all, I am decomposing even less aesthetically than the Paris bourgeoisie."

He loved to send notes to Nikulin via the *pneu* (or *pneumatique)*, that French postal service whereby

letters whisked across Paris by an underground system of compressed-air tubes, a system that must have
seemed perfect for such a subterranean man. He was
suffocating within the mask of Kiril Lyutov again. He
couldn't seem to put on the right pose in Paris. Odes-
san gangster, cavalry officer, Chekist, expatriate, or
proud Soviet writer? Kiril was homesick. "Spiritual life
is nobler in Russia," he wrote to his friend Livshits in
October 1927. "I am poisoned by Russia, I long for it,
I think only of Russia." Or, as the critic Milton Ehre
tells us, trying to make up Babel's mind for him: "Russia was tiresome and frightening, but it was also the
battleground of history. Paris was a holiday."

And I suppose it was, but I suspect that Babel was
already sick of battlefields. He had to go home. He
couldn't support himself or his family in France. It was
on his return to Moscow that he started *Kolya Topuz,*
his novel about an Odessa bandit who was as problem-
atic as Babel himself. . . .

4

BUT SOMETHING HAPPENED during his last weeks in
Paris. Zhenya became pregnant, Zhenya would bear him
a child. His daughter, Nathalie or Natasha, was born on
July 17, 1929. "She [Zhenya] carried the child for eleven
months, unless it is the pregnancy of a railroad conduc-
tor," Babel wrote to Maria. He would talk about Natasha
as "the foundling girl," but he was obsessed with her from

the moment of her birth. "I have become steadier, calmer, harder, and I am ripe for family life." He longed to bring his "little (but enlarged) family" back to Russia. Zhenya didn't share his longing. She was much more prescient about the Soviet Union than her husband, who was too caught up in being Isaac Babel, the ex-cavalier. . . .

The bureaucrats told him he couldn't travel abroad until his productivity increased like some magnificent diesel, but the productivity they wanted was a full-throated hymn to the Revolution, with an endless ride on Stalin's propaganda train, and all Babel could produce were oblique songs about his childhood, or about some whore who was as much of an outlaw as Benya Krik. And so he retreated to a horse farm, met Antonina Pirozh-kova in Moscow (it was 1932), and told her "how difficult it had been for him to get permission to go abroad and how long the process had dragged on." But he continued to live in his own little dream of a Soviet hearth. "I'm going there to meet a little three-year-old French miss [Nathalie]. I'd like to bring her back to Russia, as I fear they might turn her into a monkey there."

And finally, in September 1932, the Soviet "castle" granted Petitioner Babel the privilege of seeing his little daughter in France. It would remain the single most significant event in his life, a kind of mutual seduction that was beyond any of his masks . . . or powers as a mytholept. All his poses were idle with Nathalie. She devoured whatever space he had. "I still haven't recovered from the shock I received at the sight of my daughter—I never suspected anything of this sort," he writes to Maria on September 19, a little after his arrival. "It is really quite beyond me where she could have got so much cunning, liveliness and cupidity [from her father, of course]. And it is all full of style and charm. . . . I haven't been able to find one ounce of meekness or shyness in this tiny tiger cub."

"I have sired a tiger," he continues on September 25. But he couldn't utterly cure his mythomania. A kind of nagging yet playful insecurity would begin over Zhenya's prolonged pregnancy. "Now, inasmuch as she [Nathalie] was born ten days after the time limit and inasmuch as Makhno resides in Paris, I no longer have any doubt left that it is he who is her father."

Makhno had a special meaning for Babel. It was Makhno who had destroyed the advantage of an army on horseback, Makhno who was the first real genius of the *tachanka*. He hid his firepower in little haycarts, and no infantry or cavalry in the world could defeat his mounted machine guns. "Makhno, as Protean as Nature itself" ["Discourse on the *Tachanka*"]. He was a Ukrainian guerrilla who fought against the Reds with his own anarchist band. Babel admired his boldness and his bravery. Makhno was also very cruel—it's men from his band who rape the Jewish maid in "Makhno's Boys." He fled to Paris after the Civil War. And he would occupy Babel's mind as an unstoppable force, cruel as creativity.

Babel's daughter was another unstoppable force, and he dubbed her "Makhno"—"In the last few days, Makhno has quieted down and sometimes displays such meekness and reasonableness that my heart melts."

He went everywhere with Makhno, was her constant squire. "I have no time to myself because I must escort my daughter: tomorrow she goes to some birthday party; on Saturday, she has a Christmas party in her kindergarten."

But pretty soon Babel began to chase his own tail. He was still depending on Lyova for some magical bail-out. Meanwhile, he had trouble writing. "It seems quite impossible for me to get down to work here and that depresses me very much." He became friendly with Ilya Ehrenburg, whom he'd first met in Moscow after *Red Cavalry* had created such a storm. "Man lives for the pleasure of sleeping with a woman, of eating ices on a hot day," Babel had told him then. Now he talked of his tiger cub—little Makhno. But it was Ehrenburg who had penetrated Babel's masks, who saw beneath the swagger: Babel, he said, "was a sad person who was able to laugh."

He couldn't be without his daughter, yet he couldn't keep her with him. He'd received "a strange summons from Moscow." And his fellow writers had been circulating "[a]ll sorts of absurd but sinister rumors" about him. They were jealous of Babel, *meanly* jealous, and began telling tales about him to the Cheka, that he intended to "vanish," live permanently in the West. "I'm glad I'm going to Moscow. All the rest is bitter and uncertain," Babel wrote to Annenkov.

But how glad could he have been? "My native land greeted me with autumn, poverty and what she alone has for me—poetry" [quoted in Ehre]. But he would have to live without the poetry of Makhno. Nothing could hold him for very long, not even his little retreat at Molodenovo, where he could "handle" as many horses as he liked. He moved into a Cossack settlement, going from one isolated place to the next. "I am living in peace and warmth. . . . The only thing is that I can't get my daughter out of my heart" (ibid.). Back in Moscow in February 1934, he writes to Maria, "I think of Natasha a thousand times a day and my heart contracts."

That April, he writes to his mother about the "paradoxical thing" of his existence as a Soviet writer—"in our country, which is still so poor, I live in greater comfort *and freedom* than you and Zhenya. When it comes to apartments, food, services, warmth and peace—I can have it all." He's blinded himself enough to believe that his wife, daughter, mother, sister, and her doctor husband, Grisha, would all be better off with him in some stupendous household near his horse farm, and if not, what can he do? The bureaucrats won't let him out of their little paradise to visit Zhenya and Natasha in Paris. And then fate intervenes in the figure of André Malraux, who has organized his own "International Congress [of anti-fascist writers] for the Defense of Culture and Peace," in 1935. But when Malraux realizes that the two Russian writers he admired most—Babel and Boris Pasternak—are not among the Soviet delegates, he screams to Stalin himself (via the Soviet embassy in Paris). A Soviet air force plane is immediately commandeered, but Pasternak is too sick to fly. He's hiding at a clinic, in the midst of a physical and mental collapse. And Babel decides to accompany him to the Congress by train.

Pasternak and Babel arrive on the third day. It's June. Paris is caught in a heat wave. Pasternak sits like a ghost, but Babel is the star of a congress that includes E. M. Forster, Bertolt Brecht, Robert Musil, André Gide, Bertrand Russell, and Virginia Woolf. *Red Cavalry* has appeared in translation, and the other delegates can appreciate his "plumage"; they greet him with great warmth. He charms them in "masterly French," speaks for fifteen minutes without a prepared speech, but doesn't for a moment forget the tightrope he is on. He's giving a performance, and he has to make the delegates laugh. He talks of the collective farmer who has bread, a house, even a decoration. "But it's not enough for him. Now he wants poetry to be written about him," according to Ehrenburg.

Can Malraux and the other delegates catch the bitterness underlying Babel's little joke? They envision Stalin as the wise monk who never travels, who leads the fight against fascism from within the Kremlin's walls. "For us now the USSR presents a spectacle of incomparable importance and great hope," says Gide. Only in Russia "are there real readers"—Stalin's readers. Stalin, Babel understands, was the collective farmer and *mad* monk who hurled language and laws "like horseshoes at the head." Stalin was the ultimate poet, who used language to reward and to kill on a "collective farm" that covered two continents. . . .

Babel meets with the delegates. He performs, he dances, he runs home to Zhenya and Makhno, who's almost six. "I feel great. I find I am the father of an infant who is notorious for her criminal activities within a range of ten kilometers."

He's also planning to write. "I'll spend the short time assigned to me in Paris in roaming around the place in search of material like a hungry wolf."

But he couldn't understand that the hungry wolf was feeding on its own flesh, and there was even too little of that. He'd begun to dismiss *Red Cavalry* as a tale about horses. Like Mark Twain, who would dismiss *Huckleberry Finn* as a humdrum book for boys, Babel was unconscious of his strengths and sources, had no idea what could ignite him and what could not. The explosion of form would only come when an inner search clung to an outer one, when Mark Twain captured his boyhood on the Mississippi through Huck Finn, and Babel created his own world through the "flesh" of the Moldavanka. He could find no internal music for all his subsequent wanderings in the Ukraine, all his stopovers at a Cossack settlement. Babel's fire came from certain erotic moments he'd suffered through as a boy (hinted at in "First Love"), suffered like slaps on the face, and *Red Cavalry* was a wondrous, deepening spiral because Kiril Lyutov wore the mask that a boy might wear—he was a boy's hollowed-out impression of a man. . . .

Babel continues to scheme. He begins assembling exit visas for his tribe. "The prospects of my family's settling in the USSR are very bright now and I enriched the Soviet Union with a new citizen when Natasha was entered on Zhenya's new passport." But by August he was gone, without his family. And now his whole life would become more and more of a mask. He will travel with Antonina, begin living with her, but can never mention her in his letters, so that what he writes to Maria and his mother becomes a piece of fiction. He visits Odessa with Antonina, gets Maria's favorite poppy-seed bagels from a shop near Gorky Street, but he can't declare whom he had the bagels with; Antonina herself is a strange "cutout" in his correspondence, an absent detail that destroys the very message.

He's mobbed wherever he goes in Odessa. "Completely unknown street cleaners, news vendors and what not, come up to me in the street, say hello and engage me in the most incredible conversations." And when he comes out of a theater, hordes of young people block the way to his automobile. . . .

Even with all the adulation, he can't really return to Odessa. The Moldavanka was the land of memory, where his imagination could dwell. But it wasn't a home. *There is no there there*, Gertrude Stein once said, and Gertrude wasn't wrong. When Alexander Blok, Russia's great Symbolist poet, was arrested by the Cheka in 1919, he sat in the same cell with a bunch of monarchists and Mensheviks who argued relentlessly about Russia's future. And Blok had only this to say:

"But where will the artist, with his homeless craft, go to in your future?" (quoted in Shentalinsky)

5

Babel may have walked Paris, but he was no *flâneur*, like Walter Benjamin or Baudelaire. Benjamin was a pathfinder who could feel the lyrical pull between epochs, fall upon arcades or wounded stones in Paris or Marseilles, discover the design of the nineteenth century embedded in the twentieth. His home was the library he carried from place to place, with the quotations he would cram into every text like some movable mosaic. Babel wasn't of the same priesthood.

The two stories he wrote about Paris, "Dante Street" (1934) and "The Trial" (1938), read like bits of a travelogue, or the journal of someone stuck in a place he doesn't want to be. "There is no solitude more deadly than solitude in Paris," says the nameless narrator of "Dante Street," who wears the trappings of Isaac Babel. "For all those who come from afar this town is a form of exile." In "The Trial," Ivan Nedachin, a former lieutenant colonel with the Whites, who has wandered from Zagreb to Paris, where he couldn't pass the taxi driver test, becomes a gigolo and a jewel thief. The daughter-in-law of his last victim goes to the police. Nedachin is arrested in a Montparnasse wine cellar "where Moscow gypsies sang." At criminal court a gendarme pushes him "out into the light, as a bear is pushed into a circus arena." He is a bear, but from some unknown circus. "He towered over the crowd—helpless, large, with dangling arms—like an animal from another world."

Babel was this same animal, and not because of Paris. Paris becomes a macabre stand-in for the feeling of *foreignness* in his own psyche. . . .

Babel's best story about Paris takes place in Petersburg. Published in 1932 (like "Argamak"), it has ambiguous antecedents. Babel would have us believe that he composed "Guy de Maupassant" between 1920 and 1922. But I'd swear it couldn't have been written, or greatly revised, until after his first trip to France. Cynthia Ozick calls the story "a cunning seriocomic sexual fable fixed on the weight and trajectory of language itself." It's also Babel's most disturbing autobiography.

The narrator, whose fortunes are closely linked to Babel's, finds himself in Petersburg in 1916 with a forged passport and without a penny. He's twenty years old and he's taken in by Alexey Kazantsev, a teacher of Russian literature whose real passion is Spain. "Kazantsev had never so much as passed through Spain, but his love for that country filled his whole being."

Babel has visited upon Kazantsev his own puppy love for France. He appears like a ghostly fragment inside all the main characters—as if they (and we ourselves) were swimming with Isaac Babel in the underbelly of a dream. . . .

The narrator refuses to become a clerk: "[B]etter starve, go to jail, or become a bum than spend ten hours

a day behind a desk in an office." And this credo feeds
Babel's own mythology, testifies to his acumen as the
barefoot boy who rushes from one adventure to the
next. "This wisdom of my ancestors was firmly lodged
in my head: we are born to enjoy our work, our fights,
and our love: we are born for that and for nothing else."

But his ancestors were locked within the ghetto wall,
a pale that would have broken his ancestors' back, and
that delivered little love or joy. Yet our picaro rushes
out to collect whatever he can. Bendersky, the Jewish banker-lawyer who owns a publishing house, has
decided to republish all of Maupassant, with his wife,
Raïsa, as translator. Raïsa can't make her translations
work, and Kasantsev recommends the narrator.

He arrives at the Benderskys' in a borrowed coat.
They live in a mansion near the Moyka River. A high-
breasted maid greets him at the door. "In her open gray
eyes one saw a petrified lewdness. She moved slowly.
I thought: when she makes love she must move with
unheard-of agility."

The maid's imagined acrobatics are like the flights of
power in Babel's art—that movement from inertia into
an acrobat of image and sound. . . .

But it's Raïsa who occupies our mind, and not the
maid. "Maupassant," she tells the boy, "is the only passion of my life," and Babel might well have been looking
at his own face in the mirror—she's the erotic mon-
strosity of *his* lifelong passion for Maupassant.

But there's little of Maupassant in Raïsa's

translations—all she has is "something loose and life-less, the way Jews wrote Russian in the old days," *before* Isaac Babel.

The boy brings Raïsa's translations home to Kasant-sev's attic and cuts his way through "the tangled under-growth of her prose." And it's Babel who's speaking here, not the picaro. "A phrase is born into the world both good and bad at the same time. The secret lies in a slight, an almost invisible twist. The lever should rest in your hand, getting warm, and you can only turn it once, not twice."

All his life, Babel worked at that "almost invisible twist." Raïsa and the boy are the twin demons that haunted Babel, one pulling toward access and jungle growth, and the other toward a surgical *pinch* of every line.

The boy returns to Raïsa with the corrected manu-script. Raïsa is overwhelmed: "the lace between her constricted breasts danced and heaved," like language itself. One evening he finds the Benderskys at dinner. He listens to their "neighing laughter," which serves as a marvelous counter to the dignified Russian he studied at school. What he hears is "a Jewish noise, rolling and tripping and ending up on a melodious, singsong note," like the noise of the Moldavanka. . . .

Raïsa comes to him drunk. "I want to work," she says, while "the nipples rose beneath the clinging silk" of her sacklike gown. They drink her husband's most expensive wine. And they start on Raïsa's translation of "L'Aveu" ("The Confession"), about a coachman, Hippolyte, and a farmer girl with "mighty calves"—always an aphrodisiac for Babel—and all the cat and mouse of seduction. After two years, the girl gives in; the coachman sleeps with her right inside his carriage, under "the gay sun of France," with a sick old nag leading them along. . . .

The boy takes his courage from the story. He kisses Raïsa on the lips. She presses herself against the wall. "Of all the gods ever put on the crucifix, this was the most ravishing."

Does the narrator make love to her or not? He leaves that mansion on the Moyka before Raïsa's husband returns from the theater. But the language of his little walk seems to support the notion that he hasn't been quite as lucky as Hippolyte. "Monsters roamed behind the boiling walls. The roads amputated the legs of those walking on them," as all godlike, gorgeous women with a pink layer of fat on their bellies amputate husbands and suitors who are frightened of their sex.

Frustrated, the narrator returns to the attic and starts to read a book on Maupassant's life and work. Attacked by congenital syphilis at twenty-five. Incredible creativity and joie de vivre. His sight weakens. He suffers from headaches and fits of hypochondria. Suspicious of everyone, he dashes about the Mediterranean in a yacht, runs to Morocco. Famous at an early age, he cuts his throat at forty, survives, is locked in a madhouse. He crawls about on his hands and knees, "devouring his own excrement." Monsieur de Maupassant is turning into an animal, reads his hospital report. He dies at forty-two, his mother surviving him. And once again Babel goes into his little act of trying to grasp something prescient in the last line of a story: "My heart contracted as the foreboding of some essential truth touched me with light fingers."

The fingers weren't light at all. The narrator *and* the author are terrified. The arc of Maupassant's life may *seem* to duplicate Babel's: early fame and quick decline. But there's a much stronger parallel than Babel might have been conscious of. Maupassant hadn't been the only one to devour excrement. Perhaps he had to devour before he could create. Images of excrement overwhelm *Red Cavalry:* fields are strewn with excrement, and the old man who has his throat cut in "Crossing into Poland" lies in his own filth. Excrement is a strange, vital force of the ghetto itself—part of its magic decay. And rather than the chronicle of a death foretold (Babel's own), "Guy de Maupassant" is about an author-magician who *lent* Babel a language and a country and a totemic town—Paris— that would inspire Babel, free him to build his own myths as a writer, even if he couldn't really live there. Perhaps no town could ever match the dream he had of Maupassant.

6

The last years, the lonely years, as Stalin tightened his noose—what could it have been like for Babel after he came home from France? It was August 1935. He'd lingered for two months with Zhenya and Makhno, while the other Soviet delegates at Malraux's little congress, who didn't have a wife and daughter in Paris and were scared to death of Stalin and his phobia of *anything* foreign, returned as fast as they could. I suspect Babel was a sleepwalker for the remainder of his life, but he was still a minor deity in the Writers Union, part of a privileged caste in a "new Moscow," where "people were opening up their first bank accounts, buying furniture and writing novels," according to Nadezhda Mandelstam in *Hope Against Hope*. Babel had a big Ford, a chauffeur, servants; he could eat at "closed" restaurants and travel wherever he wanted within the Soviet Union; and he would soon have a dacha built for him at Peredelkino—but he was like a great musician being forced to fiddle, and he couldn't fiddle hard enough or long enough to satisfy his Soviet keepers.

Pirozhkova would have us remember a serene and saintly Babel, "born for merriment." But there were no more meadows in May, bisected by an angelic band of women and horses. I'm not convinced there ever were, except in Babel's mind. Georgy Munblit, the editor of a Soviet literary magazine, recalls a writer "about whose protracted silence in the thirties there were newspaper articles and feuilletons, speeches and writers' conferences, and even, apparently, satirical songs," but behind the mask of silence "was a man with an almost morbid sense of responsibility"—responsibility toward everyone but himself. As writers began to be arrested, Babel would show concern for their outlawed wives (*stopiatnitsas*), and had one of them move in with him and Antonina: "I'll breathe more easily if she lives with us."

Milton Ehre is convinced that Babel had a program of sorts, that his existence was "guided by a strategy of survival, a way to hold on in a culture gone mad." Nathalie Babel is even more convinced that her father had a program, even if it wasn't about survival. "His life centered on writing, and it can be said without exaggeration that he sacrificed everything to his art, including his personal relationships, his family, his liberty, even his life." Hence, he had to return to the Soviet Union. "I am a Russian writer. If I didn't live with the Russian people, I would cease being a writer. I would be like a fish out of water."

But he was a fish out of water wherever he was— Paris, Moscow, even Odessa, with its fairy-tale skies. We cannot tell what was in the notebooks and manuscripts that the Cheka took from him; no one has seen them but Babel himself (and perhaps his inquisitors). Their content remains a mystery. According to Antonina Pirozhkova, the manuscripts included a book of stories that Babel was preparing for publication. "And that's what I'll call it— 'New Stories.' Then we are going to get rich." There might also have been an excerpt from *Kolya Topuz*. And in a letter to Lavrenti Beria, chief of the Cheka at the time of his arrest, Babel begs Beria to let him put "the manuscripts confiscated from me in order. . . . I burn with a desire to work." He mentions an essay on collectivism, notes for a book on Gorky, several dozen stories, a finished scenario, and a half-finished play—the "fruit" of his last eight years.

Anyone with an interest in Babel has mourned this treasure trove, which disappeared when the Cheka destroyed
its files in 1941, as the Germans sat outside the walls of
Moscow. Legends have continued to grow about these
manuscripts, that their very burning was a Stalinist ruse,
that they're still sitting somewhere in the cellars of the
Lubyanka. Every few years or so, there's talk of an imminent Babel "sighting," of some novel that was recovered
from the ashes like a priceless jewel and is on the verge of
being published in the former Soviet Union. . . .

Manuscripts don't burn, says the Devil in Bulgakov's
The Master and Margarita, but even if Babel's unpublished
manuscripts had escaped the Cheka's fire by some divine
intervention or devilish trick, I still have to wonder how
Babel could have published a collection of "New Stories"
in Stalin's age of the New Soviet Man, unless he was
Kiril Lyutov again on board the propaganda train. Babel's
"plumage" —his absolute belief in the cunning twists of
language—was almost an attack on Stalin himself.

He could have polished and polished with the purity
of a Spinoza, but he was still in some kind of fugue
state. "I'm not afraid of arrest as long as they let me keep
working," Babel confides to Antonina, the same Babel
who was so curious about the Cheka, who had watched
men and women vanish. He was running out of masks
to wear and roles to play. He'd embarked on a new family, with a new child, Lydia (born in 1937), and he arrives
at the maternity hospital "carrying so many boxes of
chocolate that he has to steady the top of the stack with

his chin"—the comical Babel, the gallant Babel, the magnanimous writer-schlemiel who hands out chocolates to every doctor and nurse in sight. However much he loved Antonina and little Lydia, what about the family he'd left behind in Belgium and France? His distance from Makhno—and the thought that he couldn't watch her grow up into a magnificent bandit chief—must have eaten him alive, this man with a morbid sense of responsibility. Babel was his own haunted house. His existence had become a kind of *Red Cavalry*—a series of short takes with several narrators. . . .

7

THE LAST TWO STORIES THAT BABEL PUBLISHED in his lifetime—"The Trial" and "Di Grasso"—offer us a tiny window into his despair. I've already talked about Nedachin, the failed jewel thief, trapped in Stalin's circus "like an animal from another world." "The Trial" reads like a parable that's a little too opaque, but "Di Grasso" is full of sinews and flesh. Our narrator is fourteen. He works for a ticket scalper, Nick Schwarz, "a tricky customer with a permanently screwed-up eye and enormous silky handle bars." But these are hard times on Theater Lane. Chaliapin is too expensive, and so the Sicilian tragedian Di Grasso comes to Odessa with his troupe. Nick Schwarz takes one look at Di Grasso's folk drama and says, "This stuff stinks." The narrator has nothing to scalp; he can't even sell his tickets at half price.

In the first act, the daughter of a rich peasant pledges herself to a shepherd, played by Di Grasso himself. But a city slicker named Giovanni arrives in a velvet waistcoat and flirts with the maiden, while Di Grasso keeps flattening himself against walls. In the second act, she gives him back his ring. In the third act, the city slicker is at the village barber, while the shepherd stands in a far corner of the stage, as gloomy as Hamlet: "[T]hen he gave a smile, soared into the air, sailed across the stage, plunged down on Giovanni's shoulder, and having bitten through the latter's throat, began, growling and squinting, to suck blood from the wound." The curtain falls, hiding "killed and killer," and Di Grasso's folk drama is declared a masterpiece. He goes on to play Lear and Othello, and confirms the terrible truth "that there is more justice in outbursts of noble passion than in all the joyless rules that run the world."

And here Babel, with his usual mischief, is poking fun at the deadening art of socialist realism. Di Grasso's troupe could be likened to Stalin's own troupe of Soviet writers. Di Grasso is as much of a swindler as Nick Schwarz—his troupe has no talent at all, and it's only through one magical leap that he blinds his audience to the mediocrity of "performance" in Stalin's little state.

Gregory Freidin suggests that in the "terrifying and playful labyrinth of Babel's fiction," nothing is what it seems—opposites attract and collide, and in that collision produce a strange motif. Di Grasso is as nonverbal as the Boss, who could barely recite his own speeches, who would sit in silence for hours and draw wolves on the back of an envelope, but with his murderous jump into the air Di Grasso is transformed into a tragedian who can mouth the Boss's favorite character, King Lear. According to one Moscow legend, the Yiddish actor Solomon Mikhoels, a close friend of Babel's and founder of the State Jewish Theater in Moscow, would come to the Kremlin in the middle of the night and sing Lear's lines for Stalin, who would always cry during the performance. But this proximity to the Boss couldn't save Mikhoels. Perhaps Stalin was secretly enraged that another man had seen him cry. He would have Mikhoels murdered in 1948. It was the Cheka that staged Mikhoels' death, having a "drunken driver" run him over in a Cheka truck. . . .

But Babel's art moves in all directions at once. Even if he's parodying the idea that Di Grasso's "outburst of noble passion" (a complete fraud) can bring justice to a joyless world, the leap itself is like an act of faith: the artist has to jump into the void, can only create by flinging himself through the barriers of language into the lyricism of "an unknown tongue."

And then there's the misadventures of the narrator in "Di Grasso." He's had to hock his father's watch to Nick Schwarz. But Nick refuses to give back this "golden turnip." And the boy, fearful of his father's wrath, decides to run away to Constantinople. For the last time, he watches Di Grasso play that shepherd "who is swung aloft by an incomprehensible power." Nick Schwarz has brought his missus to the play, a mountainous woman who looks like a grenadier with shoulders "stretching right out to the steppes."

Nick is scared of his missus, who cries after Di Grasso sucks the blood out of Giovanni. "Now you see what love means," she says to Nick. Madame sees the boy sob. She obliges Nick to return the golden turnip. "What can I expect but beastliness today and beastliness tomorrow?" she asks as she turns the corner into Pushkin Street with Nick. The boy stands there all alone, watch in hand. And he has one of those epiphanies that often frame Babel's stories, for better or worse. He has a clarity, a certain distinctness of vision, with the bronze head of Pushkin's statue "touched by the dim gleam of the moon." And for the first time he sees the things surrounding him "as they really were: frozen in silence and ineffably beautiful."

But the boy's epiphany ricochets back to Babel in a manner it had never done before. Even with his father's watch, the boy isn't free. His only freedom is Di Grasso's crazy leap, as genuine *and* fraudulent as any art; and without it, he's stuck in a glimmering world that's frozen and beautiful in its silence, as if Babel were fantasizing the "epiphany" of his own death—a landscape without him.

8

"AFTER SLAPPING ALEXEI TOLSTOY in the face, M. returned immediately to Moscow." Thus begins Nadezhda Mandelstam's own journey with her husband, Osip, through Stalin's endless gulag, in *Hope Against Hope*. We never learn why Alexei Tolstoy, The "Red Count," got slapped. That's one of the beauties of Nadezhda's book. But the energy of that slap carries us right across Stalin's gulag with Nadezhda and Osip Mandelstam. And one can only wish that Antonina Pirozhkova had written about Babel with the same acumen and sense of impassioned detail. Why did she have to protect him so much? Nadezhda reveals all of Osip's faults—his paranoia; his need to wound himself—and he comes alive on the page as Babel never does in Pirozhkova's memoir. It's partly because Nadezhda was involved in Mandelstam's writing, had memorized every poem and could recite them like songs in her head. And Antonina was an engineer who abandoned Babel to the mystery of his own work. . . .

But we discover more from *Hope Against Hope* about Babel's time and the panic that must have paralyzed him than we ever do from any Soviet celebration of Babel. "Terror," she tells us, "was planned, like the economy, and quotas for life and death were manipulated at will." But it wasn't out of Stalin's own whim or perversity. "M. always said that they always knew what they were doing: the aim was to destroy not only people, but the intellect itself."

And with the intellect, imagination and memory. Mikhoels, Stalin's personal King Lear, was so full of sorrow after his first wife died, he couldn't function. "He can't forget her: he goes into the closet and kisses her dresses," according to Pirozhkova. But Mikhoels' obsessive grief—his memory—had little room in Stalin's brave new world of Young Pioneers, Party apparatchiks, and shock troops.

And Nadezhda wonders why there was no rebellion among the *intelligentishki,* or anyone else who surrendered to the secret police. "We were all the same: either sheep who went willingly to the slaughter, or respectful assistants to the executioner. ... Why did we never try to jump out of windows or give way to unreasoning fear and just run for it—to the forests, the provinces, or simply into a hail of bullets? Why did we stand so meekly as they went through our belongings?" There was "a paralyzing sense of one's own helplessness to which we were all prey, not only those who were killed, but the killers themselves. ... "

Every single soul was marked. During one year alone, 1937, the heart of the Yezhovshchina, "Yezhov's Time," when Nikolai Yezhov ruled as chief of the Cheka, 5 percent of the population was arrested. Stalin's "Devil Dwarf" *(Chyortovski karlik)* would have wiped out the entire country if he'd continued at such a pace. He was gathering files on *everyone,* even the Boss and his Politburo. As one of his superiors said about him when he was a deputy sleuth: Yezhov doesn't know how to stop. But he was only Stalin's apparatchik. He did the Boss's bidding. On one particular day of the Yezhovshchina, December 12, 1937, Stalin and his lackey Molotov examined the death list that Yezhov had prepared, checked off 3,167 names, and went to the movies—perhaps to watch an American film with Shirley Temple, the Boss's favorite forbidden actress. . . .

Mandelstam, like almost everyone else, was "morbidly curious about the recluse in the Kremlin." And he would often ask himself, "Why is it that when I think of *him*, I see heads, mountains of heads? . . . What is he doing with all those heads?" And how could Babel, the Headless Man, or Nadezhda, or Mikhoels and Mandelstam, or Gorky himself, hope to survive near a man with a mountain of heads? Gorky would be the first to die (in 1936), probably poisoned by Genrikh Yagoda, chief of the Cheka before Yezhov and the Yezhovshchina. Stalin had lured Gorky back to the Soviet Union from Sorrento. The Boss couldn't bear to have Russia's most celebrated writer in exile. "Gorky's a proud man, and we have to bind him to the Party with strong ropes" (quoted in Radzinsky). Gorky became Stalin's prisoner, with a mansion in Moscow, two or three dachas, and an army of servants (all Cheka recruits) that kept him in a kind of golden cage.

Mandelstam would die in some transit camp two years after Gorky. He refused to eat, fearing that the other prisoners wanted to poison him—which wasn't so insane, since Stalin poisoned a lot of people. It was the *urkas*, hardened criminals, and not the political prisoners, who kept Mandelstam alive. They called him "the Poet," and they fed him with their own spoons. But he didn't last out the Siberian winter. And Babel? His surveillance by the Cheka dates from 1934, when his fellow writers began to inform on him. "The writers exceed everyone else in their savagery and degradation," as Nadezhda notes. Once the hounds were upon him, it was just a matter of time. Only Nadezhda managed to escape Stalin's mountain of heads.

She was a *stopiatnitsa,* the outlaw wife of an outlaw poet. And she became a wanderer, a barefoot girl, without a fixed address. "[B]ecause I was homeless they overlooked me." Like most Russians, other than favored writers, artists, musicians, and the rest of Stalin's apparatchiks, Nadezhda was hungry half the time. "Peasants just lay quite still in their houses—exhausted from hunger. We all do this. I have spent my whole life lying down"—lying down in the dark, pretending that the Cheka didn't exist. The entire country was in an hypnotic trance. Neighbors and friends were all spies. "After 1937 people stopped meeting each other altogether." Even in the Kremlin there were no guests. Time had become a frozen wall and space "a prison ward." But there was something even more insidious. Osip's brother Evgeni believed that the real subjugation of the intelligentsia "was played not by terror or bribery ... but by the word 'Revolution,' which none of them could bear to give up."

And this was Babel's downfall. He'd come riding into the Revolution on his own fanciful white horse, considered himself a cavalier who'd throw himself into the hurly-burly to write about the Red Cossacks' last stand. And however skewered his own vision had become—with Red Cossacks on the rampage, and Polish Jews stuck in the middle of some monstrous slaughter—he was still a child of the Revolution (with his own unorthodox songs). And that's why he couldn't remain in the Villa Chauvelot. This becomes clear in his speech to the first Congress of Soviet Writers, when he talked about practicing the genre of silence. The mysterious summons that brought him back from France in 1933 had come from Gorky, who wanted Babel to help him organize the congress. And Babel's speech, delivered on August 23, 1934, may have been in a "dead language," as Lionel Trilling suggests, but is still disturbing. He starts out by praising Stalin, who had called writers engineers of the human soul, more important than tanks and planes. But he talks about the birth of a revolutionary style—"the style of our period must be characterized by courage and restraint, by fire, passion, strength and joy." Of course, Babel's songs of fire had little to do with Stalin's Revolution, but so what?

He brags about the ruggedness of Soviet readers. "Now, foreign authors tell us that they search for their readers with a flashlight in broad daylight. But in our land it is the readers who march at us in closed formation. It's a real cavalry charge"—the cavalier has climbed on his white horse again.

He speaks of himself as "the past master of silence," and says that if he lived in a capitalist country, he would have "long since croaked from starvation," or been forced by his own capitalist publisher " to become a grocer's assistant."

But the silence he accuses himself of might have been just another mask. He had to project the aura of a man who was not writing, because what he did write made him the engineer of a very different kind of soul. Like Olesha, he could find no music in factories or collective farms. Olesha, according to Gleb Struve, "had the courage to say that every artist could create only within his powers. A writer can write only what he can write" (quoted in *You Must Know Everything*). And Olesha "candidly admitted that it was impossible for him to put himself into the shoes of an average workman or of a revolutionary hero, and therefore he could not write about either of them."

And Babel, who could never be direct, who gravitated toward a crooked line, wrote a few tepid tales about the *kolkhoz,* began his novel on Kolya Topuz, the Old World bandit who became a revolutionary clown, but he wasn't searching for a new style or language, as some critics suggest; he was withdrawing into the land of Benya Krik: his real electrical circuit had always been the Moldavanka, and even Lyutov, with his law degree from Petersburg, is a creature out of this dark world. The Moldavanka itself had been masked, with its dreamlike streets, and its goddess was the boy's own grandmother, who couldn't read or write Russian, who would hold books upside down, but would listen like an enraptured hawk as the boy recited his lessons—to her, the music of Russian words "was sweet." She wants him to become a *bogatir,* which in her own confusion of tongues means a man who is both rich and a Herculean hero. "You must know everything," she warns him. "Everyone will fall on their knees before you and bow to you. Let them envy you. Don't believe in people. Don't have friends. Don't give them your money. Don't give them your heart" ("At Grandmother's").

And Babel did become that *bogatir*, something of a Herculean hero, who was never quite as rich as his grandmother would have liked, but who did wear the Moldavanka's masks and was quite stingy in matters of the heart. Perhaps he'd given his heart once, and only once, to Makhno. And perhaps the *bogatir* then had to flee. . . .

9

IN BABEL'S *Complete Works*, ON PAGE 1025, the reader will fall upon a photograph of Makhno and the master in Paris, circa 1932. There's no question of pedigree— father and daughter have the same face, the same frown, the same gentle surliness, the same truculence against the world, as if they composed a colossal band of two, complete as Makhno's guerrillas or the Red Cavalry. Babel is wearing a homburg of sorts, glasses glued to his nose; Nathalie has some kind of cloche, white gloves, white socks, white shoes, and a little coat with a cape. She's sitting on the fence of a garden or square, with Babel holding her, while she's holding what looks like a checkered bag. . . .

It was this melodic line that I wanted to revive when I went looking for Makhno in Washington, D.C. I was like some crazy picador preparing to prod Nathalie's memory, obliging her to be little Natasha again, posing with her dad, to recall the frowns below the tilted line of her cloche. I expected something miraculous from Makhno, so that I could describe that tiny guerrilla waltzing with the master in some public garden. She was barely three when Babel arrived like a Russian Yankee Doodle prepared to conquer Paris. She remembered *nothing* at all. I panicked. I begged for one little detail, a ghostly remembrance spun out of some magic tissue of the past. But I wasn't dealing with a sentimental idiot. She still had the frown that Babel would wear his entire life—that mark of the born intelligence man. And why the hell was I so severe? I couldn't summon up a single memory from the time I was three. It would be no different if Isaac Babel had been my dad. . . .

All right, I'd accept a short novel from Nathalie about Babel's final trip to Paris, a Proustian feast with madeleines and all, something I could dip into the tea that Nathalie served in Russian cups. But there were no madeleines in her memory; Babel only danced around a bit like the ghost that he was, danced in and out of Nathalie's dreams. It was 1935. "I remember the excitement of my mother, how agitated she was. She was telling me a lot about it [her father's imminent arrival]. I was both shy and aggressive. . . .I had never seen a man in my mother's bed. [Of] that I have an image quite clear."

And she recalled Babel's departure through the prism of her mother. "As excited and happy as she was before, she was very downcast after [he left]." I probed and probed like a picador, and Makhno came up with one more memory. "My mother is at the sink, in our apartment, my father is sitting at the table with me. All of a sudden she starts to cry. The knife she was using went through her hand. She was opening oysters. I remember him jumping, grabbing her arm. I must have been very shocked. . . . I remember her with a bandaged hand. That moment when she cried and he jumped. I was petrified."

And Nathalie played with her own reminiscences. "Why was *she* opening the oysters? She probably assumed all the household functions. She did all the shlepping."

Nathalie could not recollect any other man in her mother's bed. "She spoke about him all my life." Nathalie kept asking, "Why isn't my father with us?" And Zhenya's usual answer: he couldn't leave Russia and his writing. It must have angered such a little girl: *Issya was too busy with his writing to be with her*. And she would resist her father's writing for a long, long time. After she arrived in America (to teach French at Barnard in 1961), and Babel had become a magical name in New York, a man happened to stare at her during a dinner party and say, " 'I'm sitting next to an historical monument.' It was one of the things that hurt me. I didn't want to hear about my father. I was rebelling."

And Nathalie recalled the saddest day in her mother's life. It was in the summer of 1940. "She burned Isaac's letters as the Germans were crossing the Maginot line. She knew what revolution and occupation meant" and what the Germans might do to Nathalie if they ever found Babel's letters, the same Babel whose books had been burnt by Nazis in Berlin. "We lived in a *pavillon*, a little house [with a fireplace in one of the rooms]. I walked into the room and saw my mother crying and feeding the letters into the fireplace. I stood rooted to the ground. I knew something important was happening. That was imprinted in my brain. I remember the position of the fireplace in the room. I remember the drops of water on the windowpanes [in the summer heat]."

In 1941, Nathalie and her mother found themselves in the west of France, in the provincial city of Niort. And Zhenya was arrested a few months before Nathalie's twelfth birthday. The local French police had rounded up all the Russian women in Niort (a dozen or so) and deposited them in the local jail, since Russians in occupied France were considered "politically dangerous" after the collapse of the Molotov-Ribbentrop Pact. The other women were freed, but not Zhenya—the wife of a celebrated Soviet writer who was also a *youpin*, a Yid. Nathalie could talk to her mother only across a ditch. "If you don't get me out right away, I will perish," Zhenya said to her daughter in Russian, her words floating across a ditch that belonged in a surreal movie set.

Nathalie's life had become surreal. She was also alone. She went to the mayor, she went to the police. No one could help her. Finally, she went to the German *Kommandant* of Niort, who was married to an Englishwoman and was himself of French ancestry. The *Kommandant* welcomed Nathalie into his office, dismissed his only aide, and had a tête-à-tête with his little petitioner, who had all the pluck in the world. "I told him that my mother was innocent, that I had no one else, and that he had to let her go."

Zhenya was released in two days, and mother and daughter spent four years in Niort like a pair of lost birds. "We were homeless, penniless, and displaced." Nathalie never went back to Niort. "It has remained for me a place out of time, out of space, out of tangible reality." Yet without her realizing it, Niort would give Nathalie a certain strength—it was a kind of *zero degree* where all writers start, an undressed landscape where she could not pretend to hide, a black well that would free her to write about her father and herself, a reverse Moldavanka, a strange dark void where the imagination sometimes dwells. . . .

10

I was attached to Zhenya, felt she had formed Babel in some crucial way, spent her whole life mourning a husband she had lost to another country (Soviet Russia), to another woman (first Tamara and then Antonina), and to the hidden language of his own craft. Nathalie had given interview after interview, but nobody had bothered to ask about her mother. "To me she belongs to that generation of people who came just before or after the Revolution and whose life was a tragedy. . . . My feelings for my mother are overshadowed by her death. Her death is devastating to me. I mourned for years. Her influence was very strong, even after she was gone."

I wanted to know what she was like, to feel her

through Natasha's eyes. "Her friends called her 'Countess'—my mother was extremely dignified. She obviously had a great appeal to people. She was also very intransigent, moralistic, probably a little prudish. But when I was eighteen, nineteen, twenty, I was jealous [of her]." The boys Nathalie brought home "were quickly more interested in my mother than in me."

But she'd come to Paris in 1925 as a painter, and I didn't hear one peep about her paintings—we have photos of Zhenya and Babel at a beach in Belgium, photos of Babel and Maria, who's wearing a white cloche, photos of Babel at Molodenovo, with a beautiful black horse behind him, but not one image of Zhenya's art. "She never had enough money to buy paint." Much of Zhenya's work was lost when she and Nathalie had to leave their *pavillon* in Plessis-Robinson (a suburb south of Paris), and move to Niort, but Nathalie did have a painting and a drawing that her mother had done after the war. The drawing was of Nathalie's first love, a boy named Emmanuel, who was seven or eight years older than she. I smiled my own novelist's smile—Nathalie, hiding from a father who had hidden himself from her, had chosen as her first love a boy with her father's patronymic (Emmanuelovich). "She [Zhenya] and Emmanuel had a very nice relation, except when it came to sex" (that is, Nathalie's own sexuality). But the portrait of Emmanuel startled me. He had a delicate, androgynous face, with a curl over one eye. And I wondered if Zhenya had softened his features on purpose, to minimize him in a magical way, remove any male hook he might have had. . . .

The painting was even more mysterious. It was the portrait of a woman and child, done before the war. The woman's eyes are nearly closed; the child is wearing a red scarf, leaning against the woman; both have brown hair; we can see only one of the child's eyes. The sex of the child is vague—could be a boy or a girl. The child seems troubled; the woman has a hand near her heart. The background is blue-white, but the painting has its own treasure—a secret painting on its backside, a pentimento from an earlier period. It looks like a Russian village. Was it a glimpse of Zhenya's own childhood in the Ukraine? Nathalie didn't have a clue. . . .

We got onto the subject of Ilya Ehrenburg, who had been courageous in resurrecting Babel's work during the 1950s, when Babel was still a no-no of Russian literature. Ehrenburg's own career was deeply ambiguous. He'd survived the Yezhovshchina and Stalin's other purges, and should have been shot for having lived among foreigners so long—Stalin distrusted *anyone* who'd been abroad, even prisoners of war—but Ilya would become the Boss's favorite columnist during World War II, and his dispatches about the fall of France put Soviet readers under his spell. Ehrenburg had walked a much simpler tightrope than Isaac Babel. Or as Vasily Shentalinsky says, "He was a clever performer" who managed to "outlive all his friends." He was *Izvestia*'s man in Paris, its window onto the West, and could champion writers such as Hemingway and Malraux without threat of punishment. He was a kind of court jester who considered himself "Cultural Ambassador of the Soviet Union." And as Babel observed to his inquisitors at the Lubyanka, "Soviet writers when they arrived in Paris always visited Ehrenburg first of all. Acquainting them with the city, he would 'instruct' them as he thought best," like a handmaiden . . . or a watchdog.

But he was always devoted to Babel, loved his idiosyncrasies: "It was not only in his appearance that Babel was unlike a writer, he also lived differently. He did not have mahogany furniture, or bookcases, or a secretaire. He even did without a desk and wrote on a kitchen table; at Molodenovo, where he rented a room with the village cobbler Ivan Karpovich, he used a joiner's bench."

Once, during the Yezhovshchina, while they were sitting in the restaurant of Moscow's Metropole Hotel, with the band playing and dancers swirling near the tables, Babel leaned over to him and whispered "Yezhov is only the instrument." And Ehrenburg, like everyone else in the Soviet Union, shivered inside his pants. But perhaps he had a little less to shiver about. His own writing never lived near the razor's edge. He wasn't capable of cutting through the bone like Babel could. His whole oeuvre was one vast straight line with a couple of bumps. . . .

But Ilya himself was much more complex. He was a Nabokovian character who positioned himself between Isaac and Zhenya and played out his own curious dance.

In 1946, while still living in Niort, Zhenya was summoned to Paris—Ilya wanted to see her. She'd known him since her early days in Paris. "When my mother arrived, she lived in a hotel where there were many Russians. Ehrenburg lived in the same hotel." Nathalie believes that Ehrenburg tried to sleep with her. "Mother wasn't delicate in turning him down. She probably hurt his feelings—he never forgave her." And from that point on, "they obviously hated each other." But she met with Ehrenburg. And this is when he began to sin against Zhenya and Babel himself. He told her that Babel was still alive, that he'd spent the war in exile "and was now living under surveillance not far from Moscow."

Who had instructed him to deliver such a monstrous lie? Was it his Soviet handlers, or the Boss himself? Stalin was always meddling, and the Boss couldn't afford to appear as the executioner of Isaac Babel, one of the rare Soviet writers with a readership in the West. And let's suppose that Ehrenburg was also duped, that he was as blind as his own message, but did he really believe that Babel, or his ghost, was coming back?

Ilya wasn't the only messenger. Total strangers began to stop Zhenya in the street, tell her tales about Babel's life in some Siberian prison. Zhenya soon realized that there was nothing random about these little strangers, who were probably "Soviet plants."

Zhenya would meet with Ehrenburg again, in 1956, while she was quite ill, suffering from cancer. Ilya told her that Babel had been "rehabilitated," that he was no longer an enemy of the people, that he could be read in the Soviet Union, that his name would miraculously reappear in encyclopedias and schoolbooks; Ilya wanted Zhenya to sign a paper certifying that she and Babel "had been divorced since before the war." Whose agent was he this time? The Boss was already dead. And Ilya knew that Zhenya and Isaac had never been divorced. He then told her that Babel had a "second wife" and a daughter.

Zhenya asked for the name of this child, and Ehrenburg answered with incredible cruelty, "Natasha." He meant to wound her, make her feel that Babel had duplicated *her* life with another woman, giving him two daughters with an identical name, as if to rob Zhenya of her own existence. Nathalie is kind enough to consider that Ehrenburg might have made a slip of the tongue. "What I do know is that my mother then spat in his face and fainted."

11

IN THE EARLY SIXTIES, WHILE SHE WAS in New York, Nathalie was approached by an American publisher to edit a collection of letters by Babel to his mother and sister. She was reluctant at first. But no one else could identify all the names mentioned in the letters—no one else could talk about Lyova, the lost uncle in America, or Maria's husband, or the particulars surrounding Babel's "crazy" mother-in-law. And in preparation, Nathalie began to reread all of Babel's stories; she could revisit her own childhood, when Zhenya would sing the stories to her like lullabies. It was pure romance, as if Nathalie had fallen in love with her father again, though the love had always been buried somewhere. And Makhno, the little guerrilla whom Babel had discovered in his daughter, began to devote herself to Babel and all his contradictions. "In spite of my reluctance, and even a pathological resistance, my father simply caught up with me." And she's been trying to catch up with him ever since, presenting Babel with his wonders and his warts to each new generation of American readers.

The two long essays she's written about him (from *The Lonely Years* and *The Complete Works*) are marvels of their own, love letters to Isaac (and his readers) that deepen the details of his life—Nathalie introduces Babel's own father as "a man of imposing physique and impetuous nature"—but still retain the sting of a daughter who had to travel very far to find Isaac. Makhno is never sentimental when she writes about Babel or herself—she has lived in silence and secrecy, like her father. And after finishing both essays, we're left with an almost magical melancholy and the feeling that in order to complete her own journey with Babel, she will have to "return" to Niort again and again, reach into that dark well somewhere in her psyche. . . .

Nathalie's own relationship with Antonina (who's still alive as I write this sentence) is even more complicated than one might think. Nathalie first met her in 1961, four years after her own mother's death. It was

Lydia, her half sister, who brought Nathalie through the dark foyer and up the stairs of Babel's "last house" in Moscow. "I saw a woman on the landing. I looked at her and what came out of my mouth has never failed to astonish me. 'How you resemble my mother!' I blurted out—and then we both cried in each other's arms. I was amazed. Here was another woman who, like my mother, had never stopped loving my father, who had never wavered in her devotion to him."

But this, unfortunately, would be the highest point of an ever-declining hill. Nathalie and Antonina now live a few subway stops away from each other. They seem locked in some climate of distrust that's like a Balzacian battle. It was Nathalie who helped bring Antonina, Lydia, and Lydia's son to the United States. I talk of my own meeting with Antonina and Lydia in Paris. I mention Antonina's white hair.

"Red," Nathalie says, ruining my own memories.

"The woman is hard as rock. I was accused of robbing them [Antonina and Lydia]. I was covered with insults. Our relationship ended, but they were watching me like a falcon. They sent me a certificate from the USSR. When I saw the certificate, I understood everything I wanted to know" about Ehrenburg. It claimed that Antonina, as Babel's wife, "was the only heir to all his possessions and writings in the whole world." And the date on this document was three weeks after Zhenya met with Ehrenburg in 1956. "You cannot imagine the power wielded by this man. He promised Antonina that he would come back with proof of a divorce." And I tried to figure out the logic behind Ilya's legerdemain. Was he representing himself or the Soviet government in his machinations and maneuvers with Zhenya?

"Ehrenburg undoubtedly considered Antonina a more suitable widow than my mother," an émigré artist and daughter of a Jewish industrialist. Antonina had Soviet credentials that Zhenya neither had nor wanted—she was the first woman construction engineer to work on the Moscow metro; it was easier to rehabilitate Babel with Antonina along on the ride as his "legitimate wife." But however much he wanted to honor Antonina, Ilya must have known that he was dishonoring the past of a man he claimed to love and admire, turning him into a Soviet saint, with a Soviet wife and Soviet child. "He understood the Revolution and recognized it as a pledge of future happiness," Ilya wrote about Babel, the wise rabbi, as if Babel himself were just another toy of socialist realism. The wise rabbi had never really been "rehabilitated," because his writing remains problematical, with its lashing modernism that eats into the idea of any dogma or belief. Babel belongs nowhere, certainly not in the *new* Russia, which has been just as niggardly as the old about celebrating a *zhid* from Odessa who wrote about Jewish bandits and Jewish revolutionists like Gedali, "a tiny, lonely visionary in a black top hat," who dreams of "an International of good people," while Lyutov talks of blood and dreams of "a Jewish glass of tea" ("Gedali"). "Creativity does not dwell in palaces," Babel once wrote, nor does it dwell in allegiance to *anyone*—*it* exists outside the realm of reward. Babel went into the darkness and wrote *Red Cavalry,* and that book belongs to his readers, whoever we are. And in some profound way, it also belongs to Nathalie Babel, not because she's any more "legitimate" than Antonina or Lydia, but because she's the one who has continued his story. Antonina's claims to Babel's "possessions" might be twice as *authentic* as Nathalie's. I couldn't care less. I'm not in the business of arbitration. But if Babel was shot in the head in one of Stalin's cellars, with a little dirty towel to catch the blood, then the Boss and his henchmen had a harder time killing him than they could ever have imagined. His toughness, his singularity, is there in Makhno's face and in those sad "love letters" to all of Babel's readers that seem to come right out of the empty spaces in Niort. Nathalie is a minimalist in her own fashion, as brave as that little girl who danced in front of the *Kommandant* and demanded her mother's release. . . .

Author's note: "Babel's Bride: A Last Look," "Introduction: Isaac Babel," chapter 6: "Makhno and Maupassant," and chapter 7: "Final Fiction" from *Savage Shorthand: The Life and Death of Isaac Babel* by Jerome Charyn, © 2005 by Jerome Charyn. Used by permission of Random House, an imprint and division of Penguin Random House LLC. All rights reserved.

Inside the Hornet's Head
(2005)

I DID NOT STUMBLE UPON *Augie March* lightly. I gave it as a gift to the most beautiful girl in my high school class, Valerie K. Hadn't it won awards? And wasn't it about a Jewish bumpkin like myself? (So I'd heard secondhand.) I meant the book to bring me closer to Valerie, but it never did. And then, a year or two later, I actually read it and was overwhelmed by its bounty. It was a book that never stopped to breathe, and I was breathless in its wake. Leslie Fiedler calls it "unlike anything else in English except *Moby-Dick*." It had the same largeness of imagination . . . and a wondrous eagle called Caligula instead of a white whale.

But it was much more than that. It was a model and a manifest for a boy from the Bronx, a kind of open sesame into the art of writing. I'd been nowhere, had seen nothing outside my own little ghetto: all I had was a crazy babble of tongues, an exalted gangster talk, a mingling of Yiddish, Russian, and all the books I'd ever read—whole scenes ripped from *Anna Karenina,* whose heroine would have been much better served in the Bronx, where we loved tall, aristocratic women with husbands who were beneath their dignity—all the dialogue from every film I'd ever seen, which included the entire repertoire of MGM and the other majors, and the rough but chivalrous language of the street, where we were all knights in pegged pants. And when Augie says that "we are meant to be carried away by the complex and hear the simple like the far horn of Roland when he and Oliver are being wiped out by the Saracens," I knew what the hell he was talking about.

Augie's adventures have little to do with the magical places he visits—the mountains of Mexico or the plains of Paris. They are only desiderata, icons, throwaways, bits and pieces of decor in a landscape that shifts right under our feet and sends us scrambling on to the next page and the next. Augie, says Leslie Fiedler, is "a footloose Jewish boy [who] becomes Huck Finn," with his own Mississippi—a river of words. If the Mississippi gives Huck a godlike strength, nurtures him, soothes him, allows him to shove beyond the perimeter of his own lies, then it is language that soothes Saul Bellow and carries Augie March from adventure to adventure, so that he is never used up, no matter how much narrative is crammed into a single sentence. The book is a constant rush of dialogue and detail, of shenanigans and magic tricks, or as Bellow himself writes in "Where Do We Go From Here: The Future of Fiction," the modern hero is "an oddly dispersed, ragged, mingled, broken, amorphous creature whose outlines are everywhere, whose being is bathed in mind as the tissues are bathed in blood, and who is impossible to circumscribe in any scheme of time." He's a "cubistic" character, an "uncertain, eternal, mortal someone who shuts and opens like a concertina and makes a strange music."

To read *The Adventures of Augie March* is to live inside a hornet's head—to hear and feel an endless clatter . . . whose sting is a source of terror and delight. We cannot recover from *Augie March*. Its sting remains with us for life. And we have to ask why. Part of the answer is in Bellow's bona fides. Born in Quebec in 1915 (and died in Brookline, Massachusetts, on April 5, 2005), Bellow grew up in Chicago's South Side ghetto during the reign of America's most notorious beer baron, Al Capone—and almost all Bellow's male characters in *Augie March* have some kind of gangster mentality. They strut, they wear swell clothes, and they bully us with their words, which, Fiedler reminds us, land "like kisses or blows." And they capture the *tumult* of the city. Like George Gershwin, who had his share of little wars on Manhattan's Lower East Side, another cradle of gangsters (and Capone's original turf), he was raised "in the heart of noise." As one of Gershwin's own colleagues said, "He hears the noise and finds music in it." And *Augie March* might be considered Bellow's own "Rhapsody in Blue," but with a much more hysterical and alarming beat.

"I am an American, Chicago born," Bellow's narrator

insists at the very beginning of the novel, "and go at things as I have taught myself, free-style, and will make the record in my own way." We're not caught within some ghetto tale, a lightning rise from rags to riches, a celebration of America's ability to spit out righteous little citizens—noble, healthy, and clean. Augie is a monster of the New World, more American than America itself. And we have to examine this within the context of the Jewish American writer. It's not the success of *Augie March* that's startling—a Book-of-the-Month Club selection and winner of the National Book Award for fiction (it was published in 1953). But suddenly, with one blow, like a fist coming out of nowhere, Saul Bellow made "[h]is appearance as the first Jewish American novelist to stand at the center of American literature," as Fiedler says. It's hard to grasp this fifty years after the fact. But Jewish American writers had always lived in a terrible kind of ghetto, as if they were quaint little children, talented ventriloquists who were miming the American idiom for their Yankee readers, and if they were good, they might be rewarded with a few leftovers and shown off as the most current Jewish clown ... until another clown was discovered and took this clown's place. They were entertainers, dimwits, who couldn't really enter the canon of American literature, like Hemingway, Faulkner, Fitzgerald, or Edith Wharton and Eudora Welty (when women began to be noticed as writers), rather than quaint knitters of patchquilt prose. Henry James, America's first "experimental" writer, who understood the music and the hieroglyphics of modern fiction, couldn't even fathom the *idea* of a Jewish American writer. When he visited the Lower East Side in 1907, he was repelled by what he saw and heard in "the flaring streets. . . . There is no swarming like that of Israel when once Israel has got its start," he writes in *The American Scene.* He discovered "a Jewry that had burst all bounds." He worried over "the Hebrew conquest of New York." And East Side cafés were nothing but "torture-rooms of the living idiom."

James's words were echoed in every English department of every prominent university in the United States, where Jews couldn't possibly teach English literature, because they couldn't enter into the spirit of Milton, or Chaucer, or Shakespeare, no matter how hard they mimed. Lionel Trilling, the son of a Bronx tailor, and America's most eloquent literary critic, was the first American Jew to receive tenure in the English department of an Ivy League school (Columbia), and it didn't happen until 1945! The tailor's boy had already published books on Matthew Arnold and E. M. Forster, essays on Sherwood Anderson, Kipling, and F. Scott Fitzgerald, and would soon publish essays on Henry James and *Huckleberry Finn.* And he might never have taught at Columbia if he hadn't had such a melodious name— Lionel Trilling. Also, by 1945 America—and much of the world—had begun to change. The first images of GIs liberating the ghostly remains of Hitler's concentration camps had brought attention to the Jews, and a kind of niggling sympathy that *almost* humanized them. It was the Jewish freedom fighters and terrorists of the Haganah and the Irgun that finally altered the psychological and symbolic landscape, as Jews were seen as warriors rather than victims, and as "winners" once the state of Israel was voted into existence in 1948. America was now ready for Bellow's "atomic bomb." The country seemed to need an urban myth, as "relentless urbanization [had made] rural myths and images no longer central to our experience," according to Fiedler.

Bellow had literally concocted a new America in *Augie March*, with language as American as the Mississippi, and with rhythms that seemed to incorporate Faulkner, Dreiser, and Anderson, as if Bellow were a country boy and a city boy at the same time, rural *and* urban, and as if his concertina could include every strand of music out of America's past . . . except for one, that of Ernest Hemingway. In his best stories, Hemingway was a minimalist who believed, with Flaubert, that each particular sentence was an island unto itself, that the white space between sentences could contain an entire planet, and that the real thunder of a text derived from the reader's own imagination. The reader connected these islands inside his head. He (or she) was as much the creator as "Hem." But Bellow's own daring was to narrow that space between sentences, almost eliminate it, as if he returned to the picaresque of Fielding and Cervantes, but with a modern twist—the hero is as schizoid and haunted as the twentieth century. And Augie is always around, exhausting the reader with his parodies and puns, his constant riffs, thrusting the reader right inside the hornet's head, where he experienced *Augie March* like an abundance of battlefields. . . .

2

AND SO AMERICA HAD A KING, at least that part of America that could read a book. Just as Dostoyevsky had said that all Russian writers of fiction had come out from under Gogol's overcoat (Gogol had written a bizarre, surreal story about a stolen overcoat that assumes a life of its own), so American writers at mid-century, Jews and Gentiles, had come out from under the wings of Caligula, Bellow's eagle who "crackled his feathers or hissed as if snow was sliding." Suddenly the novel had burst out of its narrative skin and had become an assault on language itself, a great whooping war cry. And other warriors and adventurers, demonic jokesters, including Nabokov, Pynchon, John Hawkes, and John Barth, would soon gain acceptance and recognition in good part because of Bellow. I doubt that Günter Grass's *The Tin Drum* and Gabriel García Márquez's *One Hundred Years of Solitude* would have found many followers in the United States if there had been no *Augie March* to initiate readers into the notion that a novel could be a jungle of words . . . or a much wilder thing. Even Faulkner, the wildest of American novelists after Melville, was grounded in his imagined South, his "postage stamp" of Yoknapatawpha County, and Bellow was grounded in nothing at all. Like Caligula, his language could soar and then rocket down into some abyss. No one was safe, neither Augie March nor the reader.

But Bellow's book would give a particular nudge to Jewish American writers, make them visible for the first time, not as ventriloquists, but as human beings with a singular vision and voice that could reach across America. Bellow himself would help Isaac Bashevis Singer (an immigrant who'd arrived in America as an adult and wrote exclusively in Yiddish) with a superb and stunning translation of "Gimpel the Fool." And the fire that Bellow breathed into the story, his own magical rhythm, came from Bellow's largeness of spirit, the almost Talmudic need of one master to recognize another. Singer's concerns are less elliptical than Bellow's, but in "Gimpel," at least, we can find a prototype of Augie March—the dreamer who weaves stories out of the air. Yet Augie's world is comic, and Singer's comedy spills into nightmare.

Bellow would also solidify the reputation of a younger writer, Philip Roth, in *Commentary,* a magazine that was one of the first to value this new, farcical American voice that could often be so mocking of Jews themselves. In the late forties *(Commentary* was founded in 1945), the fifties, and the early sixties, the magazine didn't follow any pattern of "political correctness." Under Elliot Cohen, Theodore Solotaroff, and Norman Podhoretz (at first), the magazine seemed eager to experiment and to discover and sustain new writers. Singer, Roth, and Bernard Malamud were all published with a certain regularity and rhythm within its pages.

Malamud and Roth would both win the National Book Award in the 1950s, after *Augie March,* and with books of stories rather than a novel, a difficult feat, since publishers *hated* books of stories—stories weren't supposed to sell. The three of them—Bellow, Malamud, and Roth—were soon called the Hart Schaffner & Marx of American fiction (Hart Schaffner & Marx was an upscale Jewish clothier that dressed successful Jewish gangsters, singers, actors—the whole hoi polloi). Bellow would remain the spiritual father of this little club, with Singer as a kind of kissing cousin from an older world.

But there were more immediate cousins, like Stanley Elkin, Herbert Gold, Grace Paley, Cynthia Ozick, Tillie Olsen, Leonard Michaels, and Leonard Cohen, who had the same sense of danger in their prose, a crazy concertina with its own variety of registers that could play on and on without the need to end. Elkin seems the closest to Bellow in his insistence upon the mingling of high and low styles, rhetoric and tough-guy talk, and his first novel, *Boswell* (1964), is like a mirror world of *Augie March,* homage in the form of parody. Elkin, Paley, Ozick, and Roth all have a particular thing in common with Bellow—the invention of an idiolect that has exploded traditional English, flooded it with rhythms that had never been there before, given it an elasticity and an electrical pull. It's hardly an accident.

Elkin's language, like Bellow's, is a lethal weapon, a dive-bomber readying to attack the American heartland, to take revenge on a white Protestant culture that had excluded all minorities for so long (not just African-Americans and Jews), but the attack is always masked; it comes with a kiss, with a jibe and a bit of buffoonery. One can find the same sabotage in the films of Woody Allen, like *Annie Hall* (1977), where Allen's alter ego, Alvy Singer, attacks *all* of America outside of New York City; *Annie Hall* still managed to win an Academy Award for Best Picture of the year. . . .

But Bellow's attack is buried in the nucleus of his book; Augie's an orphan of sorts who never knew his dad. It's as if that monster, Augie March, gave birth to himself. "Look at me, going everywhere! Why, I am a sort of Columbus of those near-at-hand. . . . I may well be a flop at this line of endeavor. Columbus too thought he was a flop, probably, when they sent him back in chains. Which didn't prove there was no America."

And that's how the novel ends, with Augie the self-creator bumping along on his little lifeboat of words.

3

PERHAPS THE MOST LASTING and powerful legacy of *Augie March* is that it inspired an archaeological dig—it helped bring back forgotten masterpieces such as Henry Roth's *Call It Sleep*. First published in 1934, the novel slept in its own sarcophagus until all the brouhaha began to broil around the Jewish musketeers of Hart Schaffner & Marx. The book was republished in 1962 by a small press; I happened to grab hold of a copy and instantly fell into the dream of its "Mississippi," a marriage of James Joyce and ghetto English and Yiddish of the Lower East Side. I was a little priest of literature at the time and brought *Call It Sleep* to my editor, Robert G., who was about to publish my own first novel.

"Bob," I said, "it's a fucking masterpiece. Read it. You gotta publish it in a bigger edition. I'll be the editor. We'll make a million."

I was a wild child, *his* wild child, and we would have lunch twice a week at Barbetta's, a northern Italian restaurant on West Forty-sixth Street favored by Mafia chieftains and rich, melancholy men with melancholy mistresses and wives. I'm not quite sure what else Bob did other than take me to lunch. He'd come out of Cornell, had scribbled a novel of his own, and was a senior editor at a publishing house whose prodigy I'd become. They were banking on me as the next Saul Bellow, which just proves how much magic Bellow had in 1964 and how "innocent" Bob was, since every major publishing house was banking on another Bellow or two. The king had just come out with *Herzog*, which was a much bigger bombshell than *Augie March*. Moses Herzog was like a relative of Joyce's Leopold Bloom, but I didn't have the same affection for him as I'd had for Augie March. Herzog, we're told, likes to make love in the missionary position, and I couldn't imagine Augie, with all his slurpings, ever saying that. No matter. *Herzog* was number one on the best-seller list.

I was drinking white wine with Bob. I knew nothing about white wine. The novel I'd written was about an aging Yiddish actor on Second Avenue. I hadn't seen too many Yiddish actors, but I'd tramped the Lower East Side as a kid and had discovered pictures of the great stars, like Maurice Schwartz and Molly Picon, in the lobby of a decrepit theater next to the Williamsburg Bridge. Still, the book seemed authentic enough to Bob. Bashevis Singer had sent him a letter declaring that his protégé and wild child had a mysterious understanding of cafeteria culture. Bob liked to keep the letter in his wallet and wave it to me during lunch.

"That's our meal ticket," he'd say, showing off in front of the waiters, who adored him, because Bob was as loyal to Barbetta's as the Mafia chiefs. There weren't many other editors around, since most publishers, like Viking and Holt, were on the East Side, but a couple of young editors happened to be in the restaurant. And Bob would gloat with that letter in his hand.

"Fellas, meet Jerome. He doesn't write. He paints— like Chagall, swear to God."

The first chapter of my novel had just been published in *Commentary,* and these young editors pretended to have seen it. "Your kid's a comer," they said. "Roth and Malamud had better make a little room . .. Book-of-the-Month Club, Bob. Or at least a Pulitzer."

They were con artists and flatterers, and when they

returned to their table, I brought up *Call It Sleep*. But Bob wouldn't bite at whatever little bait I had.

"It's old-fashioned," he said. "I couldn't even finish the book."

A month or two later, a pocket edition of *Call It Sleep* appeared, and was reviewed on the front page of *The New York Times Book Review*, which rarely ever happened to a reprinted book. The reviewer was Irving Howe, another member of the Jewish "gangster" critics, along with Alfred Kazin and Leslie Fiedler, who'd risen out of the ghetto to reinterpret all of American literature. Howe celebrated *Call It Sleep*, and it would go on to sell more than a million copies and bring Henry Roth, who'd become a chicken farmer and slaughterer in Maine, back from the dead. Roth might have remained a chicken slaughterer if *Augie March* hadn't exploded upon the landscape and redefined the parameters of American literature; but one writer Augie wasn't able to rescue was Anzia Yezierska, who flourished in the 1920s as a kind of ghetto princess, received much more acclaim than Henry Roth . . . and a Hollywood contract, and then fell into complete silence until 1950, when she published a novel-cum-memoir, *Red Ribbon on a White Horse*, about her own unraveling as a writer. Like Saul Bellow, she'd worked in the WPA Writers' Project during the Depression (a Kafkaesque federal relief agency that paid writers to produce by the "pound"). But Bellow went from writers' relief to the Merchant Marines in the middle of World War II (like Augie March), to a teaching job at Bard College, a Guggenheim Fellowship in 1948, and to a stint in Europe, where he wrote much of *Augie March,* just as Augie claims to be writing his own memoirs while he sits in Paris.

The fact is that Yezierska fell into fashion . . . and fell out. And she never belonged to that same wild school as Bellow and Paley and Elkin and Gold and Philip Roth. How could she? She wasn't born into English, hadn't learned it as some brat in the streets of Chicago or the Bronx. Her prose would never have the elasticity of *Augie March;* there was a much different kind of hornet inside her head, the music of lament. . . .

No one really knows when she was born. It was *around* 1880. There were no birth certificates in her Polish shtetl. She arrived in America in 1901, according to Irving Howe, who documents her story with a great deal of tenderness in *The World of Our Fathers.* I would never have tumbled onto her without Irving Howe. The name stuck in my head, *Anzia Yezierska,* like a tiny, poetic lexicon that was as strange and oddly familiar as the Old World itself. I couldn't call her Yezierska. She was *Anzia* from the start, like a lost child. Howe made her five years younger ("born in 1885"), but that was the mask Anzia wished to wear—the "maiden" who'd gone out to Hollywood rather than the forty-year-old. She'd been a servant girl, a charwoman, a sewing machine operator in a sweatshop . . . and a frustrated professor of cooking. She'd studied English at night school like so many greenhorns. But Anzia was different. She started to sew with words. She wanted to become a writer in this borrowed, twisted Yankee tongue. And like Virginia Woolf, she desperately desired a room of her own. "My earliest dream of becoming a writer flashed before me," she declares in one of the last stories she ever published. "My obsession that I must have a room with a door I could shut. To achieve this I left home. And so I cut myself off not only from my family, but from friends, from people. The door that I felt I must shut to become a writer had shut out compassion, feeling for pain and sorrow, love and joy of friends and neighbors. Father, Mother, sisters, brothers became alien to me, and I became alien to myself."

Her story, in Howe's hands, has more than a hint of Jewish pathos and melodrama—a miraculous rise out of the ghetto, a journey to Hollywood, "Yiddish accent and all," a drying up of her talent, a descent into "loneliness and poverty," with a few books published "but little noticed: all in her fervent signature, pitiful in their transparency." Then her autobiographical novel at sixty-five (she was closer to seventy), with a title chosen from an old Jewish proverb, says Irving Howe: "Poverty becomes a wise man like a red ribbon on a white horse." And Howe insists that "[i]n some groping, half-acknowledged way she had returned to the world of her fathers—a final reconciliation, of sorts."

Her own father was a Talmudic scholar who totally rejected her career as a writer. "A woman alone, not a wife and not a mother, has no existence."

And Howe wouldn't permit Anzia one little ironic touch. She did indeed wear her poverty "like a red ribbon on a white horse." But the "old Jewish proverb" was her own, invented by Anzia as a bit of deviltry. What Howe couldn't quite comprehend was that Anzia was a "hunger artist," like Kafka. "She is destined to eat herself alive forever," according to Vivian Gornick, who wrote the introduction to Anzia's collected stories in 1991, when a new generation of writers and readers began to resurrect her.

There was so much confusion around such simple facts. Suddenly, this isolated priestess of art had a daughter, two husbands, a college degree, a short but not quite love affair and fling with America's foremost Puritan, philosopher John Dewey, a different name—Hattie Mayer—and twenty lost years between Hester Street and Hollywood. *Red Ribbon on a White Horse* is dedicated to her daughter, Louise Levitas, who is never once mentioned in the book. In fact, Anzia tells us in the final chapter: "I too had children. My children were the people I wrote about. I gave my children, born of loneliness, as much of my life as my married sisters did in bringing their children into the world."

Anzia was hiding, like any hunger artist, but it's thanks to this invisible daughter—abandoned by her mother at four—that we have some image of what Anzia *might* have been about. Her birth is still unclear. She was the youngest of seven children, born in the Polish-Russian village of Plotsk (often called Plinsk in her own writing). Her family arrived at Castle Garden, an artificial stone island off the Battery, used as a processing station for immigrants *before* Ellis Island. Levitas believes the Yezierskas arrived around 1890 and were immediately Americanized into the "Mayers." And Anzia, who was ten at the time, became "Hattie Mayer." Ten isn't fifteen or twenty, and she might have seized English if she'd labored in the classroom like a little bandit, but her father, a total tyrant in his religious zeal, didn't allow her much schooling, and she had to help support him and the rest of the family. Thus began the saga of Hattie Mayer as a servant girl and seamstress. But in 1899, she would opt for that room of her own, while still supporting her family, and moved into a monklike cell at the Clara de Hirsch Home for Working Girls. She conned the wealthy patrons at the home into giving her a scholarship to study "domestic science" at Columbia University, so that she could return to the ghetto as a cooking teacher with a college degree. But she had to invent a high school diploma for herself, since she'd never been near any high school.

"Domestic science" didn't do her much good. The Board of Education considered her sloppy and unkempt and wouldn't give her a permanent teacher's license. She had to drift from school to school as a substitute teacher. Somewhere in her twenties, she decided to write, and the nom de plume she settled on was Anzia Yezierska—her very own name. The truth is that Anzia had no name; she was an invented creature, a forlorn child of the New World, without a language of her own.

In December 1917, *after* she'd abandoned her child and her second husband and was living like a monk, utterly devoted to the craft of writing in this invented English of hers, she ran to John Dewey, the doyen of education at Columbia. "[B]urning-eyed and red-haired," she cornered him in his office, hoping he would intervene in her fight with the Board of Ed, and poor John "never knew what hit him," Vivian Gornick reminds us. A New England "pragmatist," he was susceptible to gypsies like her. Married, with children of his own, he took Anzia under his wing, permitted her to audit his seminar in philosophy, found her work as a translator on one of his projects, and gave the little gypsy her first typewriter. He would also take walks with her through the Lower East Side. Dewey was reticent. But Anzia clutched at him with her eyes, wouldn't let him retreat. They began to exchange letters on the sly. Anzia lived within the dream of John Dewey as some godlike creature. He worried about his "evasion of life. . . . I must begin humbly like a child to learn the meaning of life from you." She remained the hunger artist in spite of loving him and criticized his stilted, academic prose, his "clear head and cold heart." But his letters were warm and passionate. "In your letters . . . you are St. Francis, loving the poor."

The Puritan was obsessed with her, as much as his own nature would allow. "You are translucent," he wrote

while he was on a lecture tour. He began writing poems
to Anzia that he hid inside his desk. He talked about
his "unillumined duties" and "thoughts which travel th'
untracked wild / Of untamed desire."

Finally, he acted on his desire. He arrived at Anzia's
tenement, took her to dinner, and then strolled with her
in a neighborhood park. He kissed her, fumbled with
her breast, and Anzia's body stiffened against his touch.
"His overwhelming nearness, the tense body closing
in on me was pushing us apart instead of fusing us,"
she would write in *Red Ribbon,* trying to recapture the
moment. "A dark river of distrust rose between us. I had
not dreamed that God could become flesh."

The spell was broken for John. He withdrew from
Anzia, asked her for his letters back. She insisted on
keeping them. Dewey disappeared on a lecture tour
that lasted three years. Her own sentimental education was already over. The hunger artist in Anzia now
consumed her. She wrote stories that were rejected
everywhere. "The stories had become her whole existence," writes Louise Levitas. Then magazines began
to buy them and soon swallowed her up as the "Sweatshop Cinderella," even though she hadn't worked in a
sweatshop for years. It was the start of the Jazz Age,
and readers loved the notion of an immigrant working girl who could deliver the ghetto to them in good
English. Samuel Goldwyn bought the film rights to
Anzia's first collection of stories, *Hungry Hearts,* for
ten thousand dollars (a fortune in 1920), and beckoned

her to Hollywood to work on the script. And Anzia had her revenge. The Board of Education, which had shunned her as slovenly, invited Anzia to lecture on her book. . . .

Red Ribbon starts with Anzia as a starving writer on Hester Street who receives a telegram that invites her to pack her bags . . . and she's on her way to Hollywood. "I felt like a beggar who drowned in a barrel of cream." But Hollywood couldn't satisfy her own hungry heart. It was nothing but a "fish market in evening clothes." And Anzia left without having written one line. But she'd been picked up by influential journalists and her portrait appeared in all the Sunday supplements. She went to Europe, met with Joseph Conrad and Gertrude Stein, and on the trip back she decided to travel steerage like the ordinary immigrant that she had once been. But Anzia couldn't revisit her own past. She was horrified by the stench and the filth, and after one night she was transferred to second class. . . .

Still, the Jewish Cinderella couldn't last. She kept repeating her own immigrant tales. "I can never learn to plot and plan. It's always a mystery to me how I ever work out a beginning or an end of a story."

By the end of the decade, she'd stopped being a mystery to her readers. Anzia was no longer read. The Depression didn't have much use for ghetto princesses. And she would never regain those lost readers during her lifetime. But she labored continually, often spending two or three years on a single story. "I went on writing and rewriting, possessed by the need to get at something unutterable, that could only be said in the white spaces between the words."

These white spaces were her own lost language—the Yiddish, Russian, and Polish of her childhood, *before* America. This is why she was so brutally shut out. Anzia wrote like an amnesiac, with missing musical chords. And the white spaces in her stories unsettle us, because they have all the sadness of the *unsaid*. One of her most discerning critics, William Lyon Phelps, claimed that Anzia "has, in one sense of the word, no literary style. . . . In the works of Tolstoy, the style is like plate glass, so perfectly does the plain, simple word fit the thought, but in Anzia Yezierska's tales there is nothing. One does not seem to read, one is too completely inside."

And Anzia is like the dybbuk of Saul Bellow and all the stylish writers who clustered around him in the sixties; she's that troubled "ancestor" who didn't dare mix the high and the low, who was like some eternal veteran of a night-school war in which she had to spend herself to embrace the Yankees and offer them a glimpse into her private and public ghetto. She was too brittle to "evolve," to wear the mask of style after style. Anzia loved to wear masks, to fabulate and confound her own history, but as a writer she had no mask—she was pure emotion in a language that didn't really fit. It leaves us with the guileless charm of unadornment . . . and permanent grief. She didn't go back into any orthodoxy, as Irving Howe suggests. She persisted as a hunger artist to the very end, and her style of no style moves us more than that of most other writers.

Before there could be a king like Bellow, there had to be a ghetto princess like Anzia, the golem that gave birth to Saul Bellow and his flowering in the fifties. He would seize Yiddish *and* Henry James and everything else around him. He had no desire to explain himself to Americans, as Anzia did. He *was* America the way Anzia could never be, certain of himself, ready to fight any establishment catch-as-catch-can. And Jewish American literature exists in the shifting tonalities, the shrinking white spaces, that finally wed Anzia to Saul Bellow and Philip Roth and Woody Allen....

Author's note: One can only lament that Leonard Cohen stopped writing novels and that Woody Allen is much more obsessed with film than with narrative fiction. Both were once genuine hunger artists.

Faces on the Wall
(1989)

1

I CAN SAY WITHOUT MELODRAMA, or malice, that Hollywood ruined my life. It's left me in a state of constant adolescence, searching for a kind of love that was invented by Louis B. Mayer and his brother moguls at Paramount and Columbia and Twentieth Century–Fox.

I've hungered for dream women, like Rita Hayworth, whose message has always been that love is a deadly thing, a system of divine punishment. Whatever she might say or do, Rita couldn't care less. She was so powerful, she could perform the most erotic dance by simply taking off her gloves (in *Gilda*). And just when you thought you had her, fixed forever on the screen, she said good-bye to Hollywood and you and ran off with Aly Khan.

But it wasn't only Rita.

Someone must have sneaked me into a movie house while I was still in the cradle, because my earliest imaginings and adventures have come from the screen.

While I sucked on a baby bottle, I remembered Gene Tierney's Oriental eyes. She was in *Belle Starr,* and I was only three. I didn't care about the six-gun strapped to her leg. I didn't care about Dana Andrews or Randolph Scott. They were only flies buzzing around Belle. I cared about her cheekbones, the hollows in her face, the essential beauty she had. It was painful to look at Gene. She stunned you like no other star. Later I would love Dietrich and Garbo and the young Mary Astor (until she cut her hair for Humphrey Bogart in *The Maltese Falcon*) . But that was when I had a sense of *history* and could shovel back and forth in movie time and consider myself a fan. But when I discovered Belle Starr's face, it wasn't in some stinking retrospective. I had no idea what films were. I saw her face and suffered.

I've been suffering ever since. At fifty, still a boy somehow, I walk into a movie house close to midnight and watch Kevin Costner and Sean Young in *No Way Out,* a rather implausible remake of *The Big Clock*, with the Pentagon and a "masked" Soviet spy in place of a New York publishing empire (what's really missing is Charles Laughton's face). The projector breaks down during a seduction scene in the backseat of a limo. Sean Young disappears from the theater's wall. The audience begins to riot. The images return with no sound track. And we're stuck in spooky silence. It doesn't take a genius to understand how much we depend on the little noises that surround a film—the rustle of a skirt, the opening of a door, the romantic leitmotif more than the babble, which we can live without. We cannot bear absolute silence in a movie house; the shadows on the wall stop reassuring us, even in Technicolor; the faces *feel* sepulchral.

The sound returns, and I can watch Kevin Costner and Sean Young (the beautiful android from *Blade Runner*) in my usual hibernation at the movies. The heartbeat slows. I'm like a bat with folded wings. Costner's conventional handsomeness soothes the blood. He's easy to look at. A star. But Sean Young dies a third of the way through the film. And we move from romance to a convoluted manhunt. I carry around all the illogic of a disappointed child. I want her to rise from the dead and return to Kevin Costner. Of course she doesn't. It's Hollywood in its seventh generation, not Dalí or Buñuel.

Still, I get up from my seat with the same exhilaration I often feel at the end of a movie, as if I've been through a period of profound rest, no matter what maneuvers and machinations are on the screen. Those thirty-foot faces always hold my eye.

2

MOVIE TIME HAS ITS OWN LOGIC AND LAWS, related to little else in our lives. I don't mean by this that watching a movie is more "authentic" than reading a book or attending the theater or making love. We dream our way through all these events, involved with the crazy continuum of present, future, and past, which never really figured in the safe mechanics of Sir Isaac Newton, the greatest scientist who ever lived. Sir Isaac believed that the universe was a magnificent but tight machine where "the whole future depends strictly upon the whole past."

Our own century, the century of Hollywood and Hitler, has pushed us further and further away from Newton's corner. The wildness and randomness we've discovered in the universe, we've also discovered in ourselves. And not even Louis B. Mayer and his mother's famous chicken soup (dispensed at the MGM commissary for thirty-five cents a bowl) could keep this randomness out of films. He could nourish his stars on the MGM lots, groom them, reinvent their lives and their looks, but he couldn't control their faces on the movie-house wall. Those faces had a darker message than anyone L.B. subscribed to. They had their own wild resonance. They scared as much as they delighted. The simplest screen was much bigger (and darker) than any of the movie moguls. The studios could tyrannize the content of a film, declare a land of happy endings, but they weren't sitting with you in the dark. They could control Joan Crawford, but not the hysteria hidden behind those big eyes, or the ruby mouth that could almost suck you into the screen. The stars were very strange creatures. They had the power to hypnotize whole generations in ways that Sir Isaac couldn't have guessed. The stars were like the doubles of our own irrational, perverse selves. In matters of Hollywood, our feelings were often mixed: we were tender and murderous toward the stars. They were like a demonic parent-child, lover and stranger, and we were *always* involved in some sort of incestuous relationship with them, with those faces (and bodies) on the wall.

If I read *The Sound and the Fury* or *Middlemarch*, I'm filled with the aromas of either book, with past readings and relationships to the characters, with a whole continent of language and scenes, but the books don't frighten me. I can enter into their dream songs, and leave at my own will. But if I'm watching *Casablanca* on the wall, I'll let my eye slip past the phony details, the studio-bound streets, the laughable sense of a fabricated city, and drift into that dream of Humphrey Bogart and Rick's Café Américain, which exists outside any laws of physics, like the eternal dream of Hollywood itself, a little dopey, but with a power we can't resist. I don't crave popcorn while Bogart lisps. I'm a ghost "on the wrong side of the celluloid," almost as immaterial as those figures I'm watching, involved in their ghostly dance. I'm Bogart and Ingrid and the piano player Sam and Paul Henreid's perennial wooden face. We lend ourselves, give up boundaries in the dark that we'd never dare give to a lover. We are ghosts absorbing other ghosts, cannibals sitting in a chair. . . .

I can remember the movie house where I saw *They Died with Their Boots On.* The RKO Chester. It was part of a special treat. I'd gone with my uncle and my older brother. It was at night. And I was barely five. It was the first time I could link a particular movie to a particular palace, and therefore it's my first memory as a moviegoer, sadder than seeing Gene Tierney as Belle Starr, because I can't recollect the circumstances surrounding her face. *Boots* starred Errol Flynn. It was about Custer's Last Stand. I couldn't have known who Custer was. I hadn't even graduated from kindergarten. But I remember horses' hooves, Custer's mustache, his coat of animal hair, and Chief Crazy Horse (Anthony Quinn).

I've never seen the film again. But I haven't forgotten that call to death as Custer rides to meet the Sioux. It didn't matter that I was in short pants. I understood the vocabulary of this film. It was as if I'd been a moviegoer all my life. My uncle and brother were held in the suspense of the story, even though they must have heard of Little Bighorn. They were older, wiser, more schooled in the American way. But I could read faces on a wall. And I saw something amiss in Errol Flynn's eyebrows, in that dark knit of his face. I shivered in my seat and pondered the enigma of those side balconies with boxed-off chairs that never made sense in a movie house, because you had to observe a film at such a deep angle, all the action seemed to curve away from you, to fall right out of your grasp. I counted my fingers. I combed my hair with a pencil. Anything, anything rather than watch the massacre I felt was coming. I didn't want Errol to die. He had long hair, like a girl. He was much prettier than his screen wife, Olivia de Havilland. This was her last film with Errol. She was always a nub of virtue around his neck, whether the film was about Robin Hood, Custer, or Captain Blood. But I wasn't a film historian at five. I was crapping in my pants at the RKO Chester, and I couldn't keep my eyes off Errol Flynn.

Custer dying with all his men depressed me for months. It wasn't that I had discovered death at the movies. There was polio, and other diseases. A neighbor falling off the fire escape. Bombings in Europe that my brother had talked about. But screen dying is like no other dying in the world. I'd gotten used to Custer's long hair. I belonged with the Seventh Cavalry. There was almost a religious conversion in the dark. I'd become whatever Custer was. And when he died, the loss was just too great.

3

There was an actress I noticed in 1944. She played Velvet Brown, an English girl who wins a horse. Into her life comes a former jockey who was the star of the film. Mickey Rooney himself, twenty-four years old but looking fifteen. He was one of the biggest box-office draws in the world, "burying" Shirley Temple in 1939. I liked his dash. But it was the girl who drove the eyes out of your head. I'd seen her before in *Lassie Come Home*. But I was crazy about Lassie and not the girl. And suddenly there she was, the child-woman, Elizabeth Taylor, in *National Velvet*. The most beautiful actress in

Hollywood at eleven. Liz had a kind of angelic look, but the face was so stunning that the voluptuous woman was already there in her eyes, like some dark lady in waiting. She was the one girl I ever really wanted to marry. I got her photograph at the Loew's Paradise, and it hung over my bed like a love charm. She was five years older than the little moviegoer, but I swore to catch up. I'd kick Rooney in the pants. I'd become a mogul.

I was loyal to Liz for about a year. Then I took her photo down from the wall. I graduated to Gilda. Half the Western World fell for Rita Hayworth, the love goddess who was so shy, she couldn't bear to be in a crowd. She'd been married to Orson Welles, but the goddess was jealous of his every move. She grew estranged from Orson, and hired his former secretary, Shifra Haran, to accompany her on a voyage to the French Riviera. Shifra Haran had to carry ten thousand dollars in cash to take care of the goddess, who was "prey to persistent depression." Aboard the ocean liner to Cap d'Antibes Rita lived like a ghost. She "couldn't stand being looked at." She ate in her cabin with her companion-nurse and "would go walking when it was darkest, when there weren't too many people around. She was virtually a prisoner in her room."

But this seclusion never hurt her on the screen. Rita erupted in 1946. It was as if the world had woken from the war and exploded into sex. Rita sat on her own atomic atoll, with energy at the root of her red, red hair. It didn't matter that her hair was dyed, or that her forehead had been plucked, or that the song she sang in *Gilda,* "Put the Blame on Mame," was "ghosted" by Anita Ellis. Ellis would become her ghost again. She sounded like Rita Hayworth. And Glenn Ford was her perfect foil. Handsome and passive, without a touch of humor, he couldn't really contain Rita's storm. The camera didn't seem to know what to do with her face, other than record its carnivorous beauty. Gilda could have eaten you alive.

Her beauty, says critic Michael Wood, was not "an exceptional gift: but an accentuation of normal good features into an ideal form, the sort of poisoned inheritance that could fall to anyone." *Poisoned inheritance.* "Here was a sex object disassociating herself from all the excitement . . . simultaneously too ordinary and too beautiful."

But there was a deeper ambivalence. She was the shiest of girls and the most brazen. The camera did for Rita what it did for other goddesses, gave her a kind of release. She had the haunted look of all film beauties, women *and* men. She rushed into our lives through her image on the wall and wouldn't let go. She tried to repeat her success with Glenn Ford in *The Loves of Carmen.* But she was only Gilda in a Spanish veil. And as she lamented to Shifra Haran, "Every man I've known has fallen in love with Gilda and wakened with me."

She'd fallen captive to her own image on the screen, Rita Hayworth, the prisoner of sex. Husbands, lovers, alcohol. And romance floated past her like some pirate ship. She couldn't recapture her audience after her wedding to Aly Khan. She was constantly making a comeback. She tried the theater and couldn't remember her lines. People blamed it on the alcohol, but she'd developed Alzheimer's, that disease of forgetfulness. And she died in the care of her daughter, Princess Yasmin.

But it was more than the pirate ship of romance that ruined Rita Hayworth. More than her marriages. More than her fights with Harry Cohn (king of Columbia Pictures), or that poisoned inheritance of her face. America has always been very skittish about its love goddesses, as if an audience could only get so near, and then had to retreat from the fire. Look at Kim Basinger, a woman as carnivorous as Rita and even more beautiful. The *new* Hollywood casts her as one "strawhead" after the other, a playmate to Bruce Willis, or Mickey Rourke and Robert Redford. Redford sleeps with Kim in *The Natural* and hits home runs to the image of Glenn Close in center field.

Even without a Hollywood Production Code that wouldn't permit marriage beds or a woman's navel to be shown on the screen, we haven't rid ourselves of the Puritan ethic. Louis B. Mayer was speaking for most of America when he said that he didn't want "whores" at MGM. Leo the Lion could only tolerate so much of sex. Kathleen Turner can take off her clothes in *Body Heat* and *Prizzi's Honor,* but she doesn't have that hungry look. She makes love like a beautiful technician.

She's not lost in the musk of her own body, like Marilyn . . . or Kim Basinger.

We've adored our love goddesses and been frightened of them. Brando also had that dangerous look. He was some kind of "goddess." His sexuality disturbed a whole generation. He fell to earth in 1950 like a furry being from another planet. He was dark, had terrific biceps and a sensuous mouth. He was a paraplegic in *The Men,* his first film, and Teresa Wright didn't know what to do with Brando. The reality of the film was that Marlon was much more sexy than Teresa Wright. She was like a walking package around the whirlwind of his desires. And the country, which had fallen asleep again and was scared to death of communism, longed for Eisenhower and tolerated the bulbous, blinking face of Richard Nixon. It wanted mom and pop, vanilla ice cream, and searched for its heartland and the lost frontier. And into that timid, sleeping country came Brando, and Elvis, and Marilyn Monroe, with a kind of magnificent stink. They were un-American. They didn't wash the way we did. Norman Mailer remembers Marilyn Monroe from her days at the Actors Studio. Marilyn had a red nose. "She smelled dank—an odor came off her." But that odor has obsessed Mailer for life. Marilyn inhabits his head like some moonwalker, overripe, as all sexual creatures are.

And while Senator Joe McCarthy took on the State Department, the U.S. Army, Congress, Hollywood, the Soviet Union, and whatever other red and pink devils were lying around, Brando "feminized" the American screen. In *Viva Zapata!, The Wild One, Julius Caesar, A Streetcar Named Desire, On the Waterfront,* and *The Men,* he was the real love interest, and whatever women were around lived in his shadow, even Vivien Leigh. And then it all stopped. Brando became more and more mannered and baroque. He would mugger in most of his films, do a series of impersonations, like a thickening ape, until he ended up as Superman's dad, earning millions for a moment that seemed to punctuate his own invisibility. *Our* Brando had fallen off the edge of the screen. He'd retired to Tahiti, like Gauguin. But he wasn't discovering modern, magical art in those island faces. He was in retirement from himself, exiled, like the Napoléon he once played, searching for his own Désirée. Yet he wasn't that different from Greta Garbo. " I had made enough faces," she announced after completing *Two-Faced Woman* in 1941.

Making faces. Isn't that what films are all about? Brando had tired of his screen face, and so had Garbo. And for almost fifty years now she's become the phantom of New York, appearing at lunch counters, disappearing into Central Park, her romantic presence as strong as ever. Time has frozen around her. Dietrich ages. Rita dies. But Garbo's absence-presence is like a song to Hollywood itself. Does it matter very much that TV and tennis, rock stars and nighttime soap operas have grabbed hold of America? We still have

Greta Garbo, and that long, long romance of her face on the wall.

4

HOLLYWOOD WAS THE FIRST GLOBAL VILLAGE. Long before jumbo jets and Telstar communications, the world swam with Esther Williams, skated with Sonja Henie, danced with Ginger and Fred. Gary Cooper was more recognizable, more beloved, than any king or president. Clark Gable wouldn't wear an undershirt in *It Happened One Night*, and haberdashery stores shuddered at their loss of revenue. American movie stars didn't have to bother creating fashions; their very looks made a whole planet shiver with delight. We forget how beautiful almost all of them were. Barbara Stanwyck may have been the ice mama of the fifties, the Western Witch *(Cattle Queen of Montana, The Maverick Queen,* etc.), but she was gorgeous and fragile as Stella Dallas. William Holden grew surly and tough in *Stalag 17*, but he was once the golden boy of Hollywood. Gene Tierney waltzed through World War II in film after film that made me sick with desire. It hurt your eyeballs to watch Tyrone Power (one of the first "female" men) in *Alexander's Ragtime Band*. Even at five I wanted to kiss Alice Faye. If Louis B. Mayer outlawed toilet seats, if he forbade all the "natural functions" on-screen, if he got us to believe that movie stars never had to piss like you or me, he was able to manufacture an idealized atmosphere, a universe where the stars lived for romance. This was the mark of Hollywood, its greatness, and its absurd quest. I grew up believing that Yvonne De Carlo was just around the corner. All you had to do was blink and find Ali Baba and the Forty Thieves. Even Paul Henreid, with his wooden mouth, could become a pirate on the Spanish Main.

I still dream of Henreid dueling with Walter Slezak, who was as familiar to me as my own face. I saw myself as fat Walter. He was my favorite villain. The world divided itself into a long, bitter, and passionate duel between Henreid or Tyrone Power *and* Basil Rathbone, George Sanders, Henry Daniell, or Walter Slezak, over the body of Maureen O'Hara. It didn't matter how often the duel was played out. Maureen O'Hara must have exhausted herself, racing from set to set, living in one of the artificial oceans on the back lots of Warner Bros. and Twentieth Century–Fox.

All that swagger, that preposterous choreography of pistols and swords, was only the lines and ligaments of romance. Whoever won got Maureen O'Hara, or some other wench, who would drive Tyrone Power bananas for the rest of his life. Poor Walter Slezak didn't really count. The most important duel was between the lovers themselves, like Gregory Peck and Jennifer Jones in *Duel in the Sun* (1946). It was a film that destroyed me and every single equation I had about the prospects of a normal, happy life removed from the screen. Jennifer was some kind of half-breed. And Peck was the rancher's son. Both of them had the highest cheekbones in Hollywood. They couldn't bear to be with or without each other. That, I understood, very early on, was tantamount to love. If it couldn't suck at your blood, it was worth nothing at all.

Duel in the Sun is probably one of the longest, emptiest epics of all time. But I adored the sheer meanness of the film, its caterwauling, its hymn to greed, and its monomania: lovers had to crawl across the desert and kill each other, or it wasn't romance. David O. Selznick hoped *Duel* would be another *Gone With the Wind;* it wasn't. But I can still hear the ominous jingle of Peck's spurs, feel those dark caverns in his face, the lithe movements of a merciless man. Lewt, Lionel Barrymore's boy, who wears his lean saddle pants, murders Charles Bickford, and seduces Jennifer Jones. It was here that my erotic cradle began to rock and rock and rock. I didn't like *The Best Years of Our Lives* (the critics' choice of 1946), with all its little problems about soldiers and sailors returning from the war. I wanted high opera, not Fredric March as a banker with a sergeant's stripes.

And I've been lost ever since in the caverns of Lewt McCanles' face, waiting for my own love-death. Tristan and Isolde go West. But it wasn't funny, because to discover *Duel in the Sun* at nine or ten was to be caught in a state of erotic arrest. I saw Lewt and Pearl (Jennifer Jones) as a particular conundrum, paradigms of American culture and all its plangent songs.

I wasn't the only one who suffered. Hollywood fashioned a poetics of love that was found nowhere else on the planet. It was a democracy of beautiful faces, an homogenized landscape of sex. In movieland, the Hollywood of Mayer and the other moguls, there was no *auteur's* theory about directors sculpting all those shadows on the wall. Directors and writers and cinematographers were vague articles that were listed in the credits, and then disappeared. "When I was twelve or thirteen," Federico Fellini recalls, "I went to movies all the time—American movies. But I did not know there were directors of movies. I always thought the actors did everything."

And that's how it seemed to most of us. *They* were the magic quotients, the presences that held us in our seats. In "Autobiography of a Spectator," the late Italian novelist Italo Calvino says, "For me movies meant . . . the current Hollywood production." Calvino became a "serious" moviegoer around 1937 (the year I was born). "American movies of that time could boast an array of actors' faces unequaled before or since. . . . What we know as the 'Hollywood firmament' constituted a system to itself, with its constants and its variables, a human topology . . . from the broad and languid mouth of Joan Crawford to the thin and pensive one of Barbara Stanwyck." Calvino understood the legacy of Louis B. Mayer's (and Jack Warner's) exquisite circus of women and men. American films favored a kind of alabaster look, a flawless photogenic dream that " did not teach us to see real women with an eye prepared to discover unfamiliar beauty." Screen women became "phantoms of carnal aggressiveness," like Harlow and Crawford, and such powerful creatures "prevented you from being satisfied with what little (or much) you might encounter and it drove you to project your desires farther, into the future, the elsewhere, the difficult."

And I've never seemed to crawl out of that situation Calvino describes. The faces and bodies I adore have always led me back to shadows on a wall. Calvino realized the dilemma of the moviegoer. That descent into the cave isn't all out of fun. We're driven to it, because "the film of which we self-deceptively thought we were only spectators is the story of our life." And that's why we're mesmerized from the moment we enter the cave. The screen caresses our history, shapes us as we shape those phantoms on the wall; and as we watch, we discover our own design. We become Cassandras, predicting pasts and futures, futures and pasts.

5

CASSANDRA SITS IN HER PLACE. She's a little boy of seven. She's watching a guy with a cleft in his chin. Call him Cary Grant. He plays Ernie Mott, a wandering tinker and penny hoodlum in Hollywood's idea of London's East End *(None But the Lonely Heart)*. London was very exotic to a boy of seven. But I was sick to death, same as Ernie Mott. Both of us were in love

with June Duprez. She had that dark, dreamy air of a
Brooklyn-Bagdad princess. June seemed out of place as
a cashier at a London carnival, all blonded up, and married to George Coulouris, who wasn't much of a movie
star, looking like a snake. She couldn't have belonged
to George. She wasn't his type at all. I considered her a
more beautiful cousin of Maria Montez. I could understand why thieves and buskers would fight over her, a
dreamy girl like that. Cary Grant is subdued. His mom,
Ethel Barrymore, is dying, and she ends up in jail. The
London bobbies have caught her with stolen goods.

Ernie Mott lives across the street from Jane Wyatt.
Even at seven I understood that a girl who sat night and
day with a cello couldn't have much sense. She was like
some phantom idea of the good. But Cary Grant fell for
it. June Duprez disappears from the film. Ernie Mott
has his dying mom (Ethel Barrymore won an Oscar
for her role) and the cello girl. But I've been ponder-
ing the metaphysics of that film for forty-three years.
Because this was a different Cary Grant, not that guy
of all graces who "seemed a born aristocrat." He's lower-
class in *None But the Lonely Heart*, a Cockney brat without his usual flair (when we meet him he's dressed like
Chaplin's tramp). A street kid who's close to Archibald
Alexander Leach, the poor boy from Bristol who copied
Noël Coward. "I pretended to be somebody I wanted to
be and I finally became that person. . . . Or he became
me. Or we met at some point. It's a relationship."

None But the Lonely Heart stutters along for two

hours, but it haunts us in a way that much better films haven't. It's filled with a kind of patriotic bathos, a call for democracy and goodwill out of all that London fog manufactured at RKO in the middle of World War II. But we don't believe in any future for Ernie Mott. He'll always be a penny bandit. And he's lost June Duprez.

Barbara Deming, in her marvelous book, *Running Away from Myself*, feels that Ernie Mott is a mama's boy, "struck helpless before the fact that he is to be left motherless." Like other heroes of the forties, he's lost in a kind of masculine maze. Deming suggests an American landscape that is like a ticket to hell. She finished her book in 1950, but it wasn't published until 1969, when America, awakened by the mess of Vietnam, had begun to grow up about the content of its movies. No one wanted to look into that crazy mirror in 1950. Movies were movies, after all. Mayer and MGM. But Deming understood that a kind of group portrait had emerged from Hollywood films of the forties, "a dream portrait" that was filled with ghosts.

Ernie Mott acts out some secret dream of the 1940s, that male fear of the female who had suddenly become both consumer and breadwinner during World War II. But Cary Grant's performance echoes more than that. He'd come out of the Bristol slums, belonging to Elias and Elsie Kingdon Leach. His dad was a garment worker who died an alcoholic. His mom went mad. The boy ran away from home to join a group of acrobats. He walked on stilts for a while. He worked in musical comedies, developed a new persona with the help of Noël Coward. He was an established star by the time he played Ernie Mott, forty years old, married to Barbara Hutton, the Woolworth heiress.

He had an incredible comic touch, a manic energy that created "windows" for the actors and actresses around him, opened them up because his timing was perfect. But he's lethargic as Ernie Mott. He emerges from the fog with his bull terrier, comes home to ma. "Black as the ace, I am," Ernie says, but we don't believe him. There's a kind of scratchy love play between Ernie and Ethel Barrymore. She's fond of her tinker son, but she can't tell him. He's a sucker for women, Ernie is. Black as the ace, with a heart of gold.

But he seems to be walking on stilts. The truth is, Ernie can't take care of himself. He can fix a watch, shoot a rifle, but he's like that acrobat Archie Leach, a boy who's run away from home and can't stop running.

I felt stuck to Ernie, back in 1944. I'm stuck to him still. Ethel Barrymore could have been my own mom. Jane Wyatt is only one of the women I ought to have married. And June Duprez is that love doll I've followed across a thousand movie walls and can't seem to catch. Calvino was right. Each time we descend into the cave we encounter the story of our life.

Mr. Feathers
(1989)

1

THERE'S BEEN A BABEL OF BOOKS on Hollywood, in every language of the world. Louis B. Mayer alone has at least half a dozen. Every year a wounded lover comes out of the woodwork to write about his or her adventures with a star. Each major studio has an epic or two devoted to its films, its stars, its furniture. One biographer believes Errol Flynn was a Nazi agent. Another believes that Lillian Hellman, who haunted Hollywood in the thirties, might have been a member of the Comintern. If we read long and hard enough, we discover the two thousand dolls that Joan Crawford had in a secret bedroom of her house; we learn about the love affair between Tyrone Power and Errol Flynn, Gable's false teeth, Faulkner's Hollywood mistress.

But in all the memoirs and books of fact and fable there's so little real imagination, so little meat, that the constant mythologizing doesn't bear much of a bounty. It's odd that an obscure actress named Louise Brooks,

rescued from oblivion by Henri Langlois and the Cinémathèque Française, who lived out her last twenty years
in bed, a little like Colette, who hated Hollywood and
despised her own career, should have written one of the
strongest remembrances of Hollywood *and* a remarkable
book that cozens up to no one. She's as ruthless about
herself as the people around her and is also filled with
a ghostly compassion for W. C. Fields, Fatty Arbuckle,
and others. Louise is like a grown-up Alice with her
own particular Looking Glass and a heartbreaking wit.

The title of the book, *Lulu in Hollywood,* comes
from her characterization of Lulu, the restless, immoral
seducer of men, in G. W. Pabst's silent classic *Pandora's Box* (1929). Lulu is the ultimate mermaid, the siren
who "sings" destruction with each twirl of her body. But
Louise's acting is so enigmatic, so removed from guile,
and so unmannered, that when she's murdered by Jack
the Ripper at the end of the film, it feels like one more
seduction. Her sexuality is like a cold electrical storm on
the screen. Lulu's never there for the other characters;
she exists only for us, the audience that sits in the dark
like potential Jack the Rippers and cannot have her.

It was Louise, "in silence and out of her own person, who created the fundamental, the only Lulu," as
William Shawn, former editor of *The New Yorker,* writes
in his introduction to the book. " Louise Brooks is a
femme fatale without any record of fatalities." And
it's Shawn who understood that the writer was there
all the time in the girl who acted and danced since she

was a child, collecting material like the webbed fist of a cocoon, forming Louise. None of those terrible years was wasted, when moguls like Harry Cohn wanted to "interview" Louise while he was half-undressed.

She was born in Cherryvale, Kansas, in 1906. She'd come from a line of "poor English farmers" who arrived in America "on a merchant ship at the end of the eighteenth century." Her dad was a lawyer. Her mom wrote book reviews for the local women's club. Louise was a professional dancer from the time she was ten. "My father thought I had been mutilated when Mother, in the interests of improving my stage appearance, had a barber chop off my long black braids and shape what remained of my hair in a straight Dutch bob with bangs. That "black helmet" of hair became her signature, the sign of her independence, the mark of the mermaid.

At fifteen, she left Kansas to study dancing in New York. She appeared in "George White's Scandals, "and was also a Ziegfeld girl, *and* the inspiration for Dixie Dugan, a popular comic-strip character who dreams of joining "The Zigfold Follies." "All there is to this Follies racket," says Dixie Dugan, "is to *be cool and look hot.*" And Dixie's alter ego, Louise Brooks, had a five-year contract with Paramount before she was twenty. She was only twenty-one when she was in Berlin for *Pandora's Box*. With the coming of sound her career was practically over. "Lulu" began to act in B films. In 1943, she went to New York, "where I found that the only well-paying career open to me, as an unsuccessful actress of thirty-six, was that of a call girl."

But she was too proud to perform in bed. And so she was a salesgirl at Saks: Dixie Dugan takes a fall. It lasted two years. Then she became involved with three different millionaires, but Louise wouldn't marry them. She fell into a deep funk. "There was no point in throwing myself into the East River, because I could swim."

She moved to Rochester in 1956, at the invitation of James Card, curator of Eastman House, who admired Louise. Except for a trip to Paris, financed by the Cinémathèque for its "Hommage à Louise Brooks" in 1958, she remained a recluse. "I have lived in virtual isolation, with an audience consisting of the milkman and a cleaning woman." That's when Louise became her own kind of Colette. She would write and "disintegrate happily in bed with my books, gin, cigarettes, coffee, bread, cheese, and apricot jam."

2

HOLLYWOOD, FOR LOUISE, "was like a terrible dream I have—I am lost in the corridors of a big hotel and I cannot find my room. People walk past me as if they can not see or hear me. So first I ran away from Hollywood and I have been running away ever since."

But that merciless gift of hers clung to Hollywood no matter how far she ran. "My life has been nothing," Louise said, but that was the camouflage of the writer who has to live inside an abyss of her own making. Movieland had become her dream material; and she was eloquent about what she hated. Not even Scott Fitzgerald or Nathanael West took us as close to the bloody heart of Hollywood. Louise had a wisdom that had come from all that desperate dancing she did. Fitzgerald hadn't been a movie idol. He revealed Monroe Stahr to us as a mythic movie mogul, but he couldn't go through the Looking Glass, like Louise. Louise didn't believe in romance. "Staring down at my name in lights on the marquee of the Wilshire Theatre was like reading an advertisement of my isolation."

She recognized the essence of Fatty Arbuckle after he was run out of Hollywood for having "supposedly" raped actress Virginia Rappe. He was reduced to directing a series of shorts under another name. "He sat in his chair like a dead man. He had been very nice and sweetly dead ever since the scandal that ruined his career."

She also understood the sheer misery behind the myth of W. C. Fields as the meanest man in town. Fame hadn't "distorted Fields. It was sickness and the clutching fear of being discarded to die on the Hollywood rubbish heap."

And she remembered the Bogart who wasn't "a cinematic saint." He was as lethargic and isolated as Louise. A "fundamental inertia had always menaced his career." Bogart's lisp became an acquired thing, since "too much dialogue betrayed the fact that his miserable theatrical training had left him permanently afraid of words." But with *Casablanca,* Bogey was now big business. Enter Lauren Bacall, "his perfect screen partner, as seductive as Eve, as cool as the serpent."

Then there was John Wayne, the cowboy star of Louise's last picture, *Overland Stage Raiders* (1938). Louise was thirty-two at the time and all but finished as a Hollywood actress. She had no reason to be pleasant or kind to another cowboy. Her own great-grandfather John Brooks had suffered at the hands of cowboys, who "ran wild in a mindless fury of boozing, whoring and gun fighting." Only ex–buffalo hunters, hired as professional killers, could stop the cowboys.

And so, when she arrived on the ranch "where Republic shot all its Westerns," she happened to see a cowboy who was a whole head higher than Louise. "Looking up at him I thought, this is no actor but the hero of all mythology miraculously brought to life."

He was the Duke of wisdom, the wild man of the West. He could authenticate an entire genre with one of his very long frowns. Watch him in *The Searchers* (1956), where he reveals an anger and a meanness that undercut his very own legend. He's as bitter as prairie dust. Proud, blind, and brilliant, with his own private country of hate. You can't take your eyes off the Duke. . . .

Louise's sense of worthlessness in movieland, the assumption that beautiful women weren't born to think, but could only become the "Big Joke," the mermaid with the mind of cotton, was enforced by the men around her. Louise felt like an idiot in the company of Herman Mankiewicz, who dawdled with her and gave her books to read. Louise would scribble book reports (like her mother), while Mank's friends ogled the "furniture" of her body.

3

CRITIC ROLAND JACCARD WROTE that other stars were "phantoms dressed in borrowed light and reduced to male and female objects," while Louise was "the only actress in film history who continually rebelled against this kind of conformist idolatry." The star as anti-star. Many people, according to William Shawn, "think she possesses an erotic eloquence unmatched by that of any other woman ever to have appeared on the screen."

Or, as Henri Langlois said, "There is no Garbo. There is no Dietrich. There is only Louise Brooks."

Lulu had a different idea.

She sensed Garbo's worth, the cruel efficient power of that photogenic face. "From the moment *The Torrent* [Garbo's first American film] went into production, no contemporary actress was ever again to be quite happy in herself." And Lulu was able to catch the particulars of Garbo's screen persona and her greatness. "Garbo is all movement. First she gets the emotion, and out of the emotion comes the movement and out of the movement comes the dialogue. She's so perfect that people say she can't act. People would much rather see someone like Peter Sellers performing than see real acting, which is intangible."

Garbo's favorite director, Clarence Brown, also had a feeling for this sense of the intangible. "She [Garbo] had this remarkable ability to register thought and emotion without doing much of anything. You couldn't see it on the floor, but on screen it came across. I can't explain it—it just happened. That's the Garbo mystery."

It doesn't mean that Lulu wrote fan letters to Greta Garbo. "Every actor has a natural animosity toward every other actor, present or absent, living or dead."

Who else but Louise, the outcast, would have dared admit that? She was so much more than a mermaid and a haunting presence. She was a chronicler who liked to paint herself out of the picture. She called herself "a born loser, who was temporarily deflected from the hermit's path by a career in the theatre and films." But while she rocked in her own isolation cell, Louise missed nothing. She caught Hollywood's clockwork, every single one of its laws. "Old pictures were bad pictures. Pictures were better than ever. An actor was only as good as his last picture. These three articles of faith were laid down by the producers, and business was conducted in a manner to prove them."

That didn't prevent Louise from piercing the mask Hollywood loved to wear, and intuiting the magic beyond much of that mask. "The great art of films does not consist in descriptive movement of face and body, but in the movements of thought and soul transmitted in a kind of intense isolation."

Louise had brought us back to Plato's cave. Prisoners looking at shadows on the wall, while their souls catch fire. Ours was the century of isolation, because all the old fabrics—family, kingdom, country, God—had begun to unravel. And the face we saw in the mirror frightened us. It was a cinematic face, both hot and cold, with the murderous look of the dreamer. Lulu? Jack the Ripper? The people we meet in our daily lives look oddly familiar, like distant doubles of people we'd met before in some movie house we can no longer recall.

It happened to Louise herself, that curious dance of an image doubling back upon itself. She'd come to the Ambassador Hotel in L.A. to meet the boy king and his queen: Scott and Zelda. It was 1927, long before Fitzgerald became a screenwriter, so his capital was much higher in Hollywood. They were the perfect cinematic couple, Zelda and Scott. "They were sitting close together on a sofa, like a comedy team, and the first thing that struck me was how *small* they were. I had come to see that genius writer, but what dominated the room was the blazing intelligence of Zelda's profile. It shocked me. It was the profile of a witch."

4

Langlois might have resurrected Lulu in France, but she was still an unremembered ghost in the United

States, bedridden with arthritis, living on gin and apricot jam, all alone in her Rochester retreat, until drama critic Kenneth Tynan tracked her down like some kind of detective-angel and wrote about Lulu in *The New Yorker* ("The Girl in the Black Helmet," June 11, 1979). It was one of those glorious occasions when the written word produces its own thunder that starts to echo and doesn't stop. Tynan recapitulated Lulu's whole career, from the dancing tyke to her days as Dixie Dugan, from Paramount to Pabst, from Saks Fifth Avenue to self-exile. It's a tale of enormous courage, devoted to what Louise herself calls the "cruel pursuit of truth and excellence." And Louise would never be unknown again. It took the Cinémathèque Française and several English film historians and critics—Kevin Brownlow, David Thomson, and Kenneth Tynan—to reveal Louise to us, her American audience, who had developed amnesia about *all* silent films.

"So it is," Louise says, "that my playing of the tragic Lulu with no sense of sin remained generally unacceptable for a quarter of a century." And it is this modern Lulu, this Lulu without tears, that we meet in "The Girl in the Black Helmet."

She flirts with Tynan. "Are you a variation of Jack the Ripper, who finally brings me love that I'm prevented from accepting—not by the knife but by old age? You're a perfect scoundrel, turning up like this and wrecking my golden years!"

But Louise had said on several occasions that she'd

never loved a soul. "And if I *had* loved a man, could I have been faithful to him? Could he have trusted me beyond a closed door? I doubt it."

She saw herself as the prodigal daughter, the dancing idiot who belonged to nothing and no one. "Remember when the prodigal son returned the father said, 'He was lost, and is found.' It was the father who *found* the lost son. Somehow I have missed being found."

She had a sad adventure when she was nine, a misadventure that would shape her erotic life. There was an old bachelor in Cherryvale, a certain Mr. Feathers, who liked Louise. He would take her to the flickers and buy her candy and toys. She'd blanked him out of her mind for years and years, until a former neighbor from Cherryvale sent her a photo of Mr. Feathers, "a nice-looking gray-haired man of about fifty holding the hand of a little girl—me." And then that forgotten moment came back. "When I was nine years old, Mr. Feathers molested me sexually. . . . I've often wondered what effect Mr. Feathers had on my life. He must have had a great deal to do with forming my attitude toward sexual pleasure. For me, nice, soft, easy men were never enough—there had to be an element of domination— and I'm sure that's all tied up with Mr. Feathers."

Feathers had become Louise's bête noire and desideratum, the dream lover who could destroy Lulu and satisfy her. One more Jack the Ripper. And the primordial dad who missed finding Lulu for so many years.

She scribbled her memoirs, called it "Naked on

My Goat," and then destroyed the manuscript, tossed it down her incinerator. Louise could not " unbuckle the Bible Belt" she'd been born into, the land of Mr. Feathers, of Cherryvale farmers and lawyers and women's clubs . . . book reports and "incest in the barn." Instead of "Naked on My Goat," we have the girl in the black helmet and Lulu's little portraits of Hollywood itself and her life as a reader rather than an actress. Her mother died in 1944, but "she never abandoned me. . . . Each time I read, it's as if I were reading over her shoulder, and learning the words, just like when she read out loud from *Alice in Wonderland*."

And so that woman with a boy's chest and a dancer's powerful legs has entered our consciousness in the eighties with her own sort of vengeance. Lulu died in 1985, as much a hermit as ever, but with her silvery, silent movements of sixty years ago *and* her words on the page, she's become our very own Jack the Ripper, "molesting" us and reminding us, too, how perverse the idea of pleasure is. A whole new generation has fallen in love with Louise, but she taunts us with her absence-presence and the extraordinary arc of her mind.

We've had Hollywood memoirs by David Niven, Mary Astor, Bette Davis, Gloria Swanson, Lauren Bacall, etc., etc.—some of them good, some of them bad—but none has seized the "flesh" of that place and the sad, ghostly aura of movie people. No one but Louise could have said that Margaret Sullavan's voice "was exquisite and far away . . . like a voice singing in the snow." Or that Chaplin was a perpetual-motion machine, "always standing up as he sat down, and going out as he came in." And when William Randolph Hearst's mistress, Marion Davies, moved with her fourteen-room bungalow from MGM to Warner Bros., it was "like leaving a palace for a stable."

Louise was never false, even about those who praised her. If *Cahiers du Cinéma* had "discovered" Louise, that didn't prevent her from saying, "I think the auteur theory of *Cahiers du Cinéma* is crap; I read the first English issue. It took me two hours and three dictionaries . . . to find out what everybody has known since the beginning of films: that some writers and some directors are jealous of the stars' glory and the auteur theory is just another attempt to wipe the stars off the screen with words."

5

WHY IS IT THAT POOR JEAN SEBERG reminds me of Louise? They had little in common, except that both of them had come out of the Midwest. And Seberg wore a "blond helmet" in Godard's *Breathless*. She was also an antistar, in a way. Otto Preminger had found her at seventeen, after an enormous search, plucked her out of college to be his Saint Joan. He was always discovering people. And *Saint Joan* (1957) should have been one more of his megahits. Graham Greene had adapted Bernard Shaw's play about Joan.

And Preminger surrounded Seberg with Anton Walbrook, John Gielgud, and Richard Todd. But the film was ponderous and silly and Seberg was out of place in fifteenth-century France. Otto the Terrible was as stubborn as ever. He put Seberg in a second film, *Bonjour Tristesse* (1958). And then Seberg settled in France. But she could never recapture that excitement or the publicity of a seventeen-year-old at the point of stardom before her first film was ever released. I wish I could say I'd spoken to Otto about Jean Seberg (I worked for him once upon a time). She'd fallen out of my memory, like some frozen thing. And then, in 1979, there was the obit. Saint Joan had killed herself. And the story behind her suicide grew into something grimmer than any film noir. She'd taken an overdose of barbiturates in the back seat of her car. She was forty years old. She'd supported the Black Panthers in the sixties, and the FBI wanted to make her pay for it. J. Edgar Hoover had his Los Angeles office plant rumors in 1970 that Seberg, who was seven months pregnant at the time and married to French novelist Romain Gary, had been having an affair with a prominent Panther, and that *he* was the "Papa" of the child. Shortly after the rumors spread, Seberg went into premature labor and "gave birth to a dead baby, a white female."

"Jean became psychotic," her husband said. She tried to take her life every year "on the anniversary of this stillbirth." She succeeded in 1979.

But I wonder if her psychosis had been helped

along without the FBI. She'd been a kind of object lesson in failure ever since *Saint Joan:* the star who didn't become a star, like a deadly fairy tale. Galatea gone bad. The Iowa princess who got turned into a duck.

By the time she appeared in *Breathless,* she looked like Saint Joan lost in a dream. She's Patricia, a young *new-yorkaise* who's supposed to be studying at the Sorbonne. She's a sometime journalist who sells *The New York Herald Tribune* in the streets of Paris and has taken up with Michel Poiccard (Jean-Paul Belmondo), a car thief. Michel has murdered a motorcycle cop, and the whole of Paris is looking for him. Godard fashioned his own meandering thriller from the sensibilities of the Hollywood B film. But there's a crucial difference. The B's never thrived on such ambiguity and disorder. Hollywood's Poverty Row still had some pretentions. Republic and Monogram liked to think of themselves as smaller, frugal versions of Paramount and MGM.

Godard wanted to exploit the actual chaos of filmmaking. His cops float like kites across Paris. His camera sways like a drunken boat. Godard himself appears in the film as an anonymous man who recognizes Michel and tries to sic the police on him. But no one seems able to catch Michel. He has a curious cloak of invisibility.

Belmondo is lean as electrical wire. His crooked nose lends him a handsomeness that a more conventional face could never have. He's like a knife suddenly come alive. But he's oddly passive with Patricia. "It's foolish . . . but I love you."

Nothing seems to register on her face. She's some kind of Lulu without fun. She sleeps with a journalist to get in his good graces, but she dawdles with Michel.

"You look like a Martian," he says.

And it's true. The image that stares back at us from the mirror is blank, like a lovely doll that has no depths to conceal. She betrays Michel. "I don't want to be in love with you. That's why I called the police."

Michel has time to run. But he won't. "I can't stop thinking of her," he says.

Michel dies, and Patricia stands over him, runs her fingernail across her lip, like a clown imitating Michel. She isn't mean. She's simply a girl without much of a persona. "I'm scared and surprised at the same time." Like a wounded animal, or a clockwork child.

How much of Patricia was there in Jean Seberg . . . or Saint Joan? Her performance is much more frightening now than it must have been in 1960. Belmondo is Belmondo, after all. Watching him on French TV in 1987, I could still recognize Michel Poiccard underneath all the jowls, that quality of being rooted in his own physical presence. But Saint Joan didn't have that charm. Seberg was twenty-one when she played Patricia. And there were premonitions of the woman who had already worn one mask too many.

It's foolish to say that Hollywood killed her. But she couldn't quite recover from *Saint Joan:* the ingenue living in a country of glass. The sad thing is that she *was* Saint Joan, but the voices she heard had nothing to do with God or the fate of France. Preminger had picked the right actress. She did have the frozen, dreamy eyes of a saint who could lead an army into battle. But it would have taken Godard or Brecht (he died in 1956) to have sensed that powerful ice in Jean Seberg. She sank under all the historic armor of Preminger's *Joan*. She was famous as a flop. Would she have survived without all that hurly-burly? God knows, she might have had more of a chance.

Black Diamond
(1978)

SOMETIME DURING MY BASEBALL-CRAZY child-hood in the 1940s, when I was feverish about the Big Cat, Johnny Mize, and played out an entire Giants' schedule in my head, I heard of a baseball player who had nothing to do with the National or American League. His name was Josh Gibson, and he was supposed to be another Babe Ruth. Josh was black, but he could still play for the Giants. The Dodgers got Jackie Robinson. Why couldn't the Giants have Josh? Was he alive or dead? Nobody knew. Stories would come to me. Josh hit a thousand home runs in the league he played for, a league of black men. Infielders had to duck under his line drives, or lose their brains to Josh. The black Babe Ruth could tear a man's head off with that mean sock of his. Josh had all the mystery of someone you could never trace.

That mystery is now beginning to disappear. William Brashler, a novelist born in 1947, has written the first biography of the black Babe Ruth, *Josh Gibson: A Life in the Negro Leagues* (1978). It comes eight years after Robert W. Peterson's classic study of Negro baseball, *Only the Ball Was White*. Peterson devotes a chapter to Josh, but he creates the legend of a moon-faced laughing giant who developed bad knees and happened to die of a stroke at the age of thirty-five. William Brashler helps to cut through that legend and give us a sense of Josh's life, in and out of baseball.

Gibson was born in a tiny Georgia village on December 21, 1911, the son of a sharecropper. The family moved to Pittsburgh when Josh was twelve. According to Peterson, he was a boy who "thought nothing of strapping on roller-skates and skating six miles down-river" to watch a ball game. But he never got past the ninth grade. He had, Brashler tells us, "a single-minded, stilted life." He was a catcher on the Crawford Colored Giants, a semi-pro club, by the time he was seventeen. In 1930, he joined the Homestead Grays, professional barnstormers who dominated Negro baseball in and around Pittsburgh. He made a local girl pregnant that year, and he married her. His bride, Helen Mason, was seventeen. She gave birth to twins, a boy and a girl, but she went into convulsions, "and a few hours later her heart gave out and she was dead."

So Josh was a husband, a father, and a widower at eighteen, and a "fledgling Homestead Gray." Helen's family cared for the twins, while Josh went back to the Grays. He hit seventy-five home runs in 1931, the year before he was twenty. And the legend of "Josh" began to percolate through the Negro leagues. He was six two, and he loved to gulp quarts of vanilla ice cream. He wasn't left-handed, like the Babe. Josh was a righty, with a short, powerful swing. He didn't have to wade into the ball and commit his entire body, twisting himself into a corkscrew whenever he struck out. Josh's power came from "arms, shoulders, and back muscles so awesome that he didn't need the coiled power of his legs or the whiplike action of his wrists." The Babe's home runs were usually long fly balls. Josh's were "quick, smashing blows that flew off the bat and rushed out of the stadium."

In 1932, he jumped to a new club, the Crawfords, which would soon become the darlings of Pittsburgh, with Josh and Satchel Paige. For the next thirteen years, Josh played summer and winter, often moving from club to club, in the volatile, homeless world of Negro baseball. He played in Mexico, Cuba, Puerto Rico, the Dominican Republic, and throughout the United States. He suffered a strange decline around 1942, what Brashler calls "a depressed and dark season of the mind and body." He became "an old catcher with ravaged knees."

Josh had a series of nervous breakdowns, beginning in 1943. The sense of raw power was gone. He "appeared glum, almost sullen, with drooping, lazy eyelids and a look of utter exhaustion." He had to be put in institutions more than once. For a while, he lived at St. Elizabeth's Hospital in Washington, D.C., coming out to play baseball on weekends. He began to hear voices. His teammates caught him "sitting alone . . . engaged in a conversation" with Joe DiMaggio: "C'mon, Joe, talk to me, why don't you talk to me? . . . Hey, Joe DiMaggio, it's me, you know me: Why don't you answer me? Huh, Joe? Huh? Why not?"

He stopped playing altogether near the end of 1946, suffering from blackouts, headaches, and battered knees. On January 19, 1947, he went to a movie theater, fell unconscious, and was taken to his mother's house, where he died early in the morning.

Brashler demystifies the legend of Josh, shows us some of the sadness behind the moonfaced mask, the disappointments, and the many spills. But the story is deeper than the storyteller. Brashler is unwilling to enter into that "dark season" he talks about, the interior of Josh's nightmare world. He tells us Josh was "not one to brood" over the fact that he would never play in the major leagues, "or feel that he had been slighted, or cheated, or victimized." Perhaps it's true that "Josh himself had no idea of the demons that possessed him, of the voices he heard. . .the shadows, the echoes, the forms he thought he saw." But it doesn't take a wizard to guess at what those demons might have been.

Nowhere does Brashler mention the rage that Josh must have felt, that horrible sense of being unmanned, of having to remain a boy playing in a boy's league. Josh wasn't the only black ballplayer to hear voices.

Brashler informs us of another case: Rube Foster, the "black Cy Young." Foster was one of the first real organizers of Negro baseball. Like Josh, he "suffered severe delusions." He thought "a World Series was in progress and he was needed to pitch."

Rube Foster pitched that World Series in his head; Josh talked to Joe DiMaggio. Both were hungry, powerful, frustrated men who turned their anger inward and used it to whip themselves. Rube Foster never got the call to pitch in any World Series, and Josh never played with Joe DiMaggio. DiMaggio, the new Babe Ruth, wouldn't "recognize" Josh, or reveal himself. "Why don't you answer me? Huh, Joe? Huh? Why not?"

Put aside for a moment all the indignities that accrued to black men after their careers were over: their existence as janitors, factory workers, and bums, if they managed to survive. Josh didn't even live to become a janitor. But let's think of something else, apart from any color ban or unwritten rule of baseball. White, black, or brown, Josh was an extraordinary athlete who wasn't allowed to enter "organized" baseball and play with the very best. He had to define himself against a patchwork, inferior league. Under those conditions, I would want to kill.

Josh hurt no one but himself. This was the rule of Negro baseball: a wound so deep it was barely recognizable. Some men talked to themselves, some men played until they dropped, some men turned to clowning. That's the advantage Satchel Paige had over Josh. Satch learned how to psych himself. He had his fluttering "pea ball," which could disappear right under the batter's nose. But that wasn't enough. Satch began to shuffle and entertain. He put himself apart from other ballplayers, developed a rubbery look to please the crowd. He could enter the major leagues when he was well into his forties, because Satch always brought in the fans. He could go back to barnstorming in his fifties, after he lost some of that magic appeal, and pitch in his sixties for any woebegotten team that could afford his price.

But Josh lacked Paige's survival kit. He didn't know how to bend. Still, his demons weren't peculiar to him: baseball itself was a kind of virulence, a distinctly American disease, with its own system of punishments and rewards; a game that men played in striped or unstriped pajamas, with petty, irrational gods who presided over a catalogue of written and unwritten rules that were in themselves a form of insanity. The gods declared that Indians and "white" Cubans could play, but not black men. Blacks had to play on separate teams.

A curious echoing went back and forth between the Negro Leagues and organized baseball, a copying of styles, fetishes, and dreams. Negro baseball had its own National and American Leagues, with a World Series that was often a sham, because teams would drop out in the middle of a season, or jump from one division to the next. Yet the Negro leagues dreamed up the idea of an All-Star Game and developed the notion of playing baseball at night.

There was often a camaraderie between black and white players. They would hit and pitch against one another on barnstorming trips after the regular season was over, and even coexist on the same teams in Mexico City, San Juan, or Havana. This camaraderie didn't occur without some kind of schism among the major leaguers themselves. The Dean brothers, Dizzy and Paul, always barnstormed with Negro clubs. But Al Simmons, star of the Philadelphia Athletics, would have nothing to do with blacks, on or off the field. And Babe Ruth, who did play against blacks, was terrified of the word "nigger," as Robert W. Creamer tells us in *Babe: The Legend Comes to Life*. The Giants mocked Ruth without mercy during the World Series of 1922, calling him "nigger lips" and "baboon." After the third game, Ruth went into the Giants' clubhouse to growl and warn his enemies not to say "nigger" anymore: "Don't get me wrong, fellows. I don't mind being called a prick or a cock-sucker or things like that. I expect that. But lay off the personal stuff."

And what about the blacks? They lived in a partitioned world of tricky passageways and narrow entrance and exit points. They could use Forbes Field when the Pirates were out of town, but they weren't permitted inside the locker rooms; they could play against Ruth and Gehrig in Havana, but not in a major-league park. Josh hit longer home runs in Yankee Stadium than any Yankee ever did. But who saw his homers? Black players and fans made a legend out of him, because Josh was one of the few heroic parts of that pathetic piece of baseball they had in the lost landscape of the Negro Leagues, a distorted melody of funhouse mirrors, great sadness, and comical masks, a black diamond all their own.

Author's note: Reprinted from *The New York Review of Books*, August 17, 1978, with the kind permission of the publisher.

Portrait of the Young Artist
as an Anteater–In the Bronx
(2003)

F OR A LITTLE WHILE, IN THE THICK of World War
II, I lived one block east of the Grand Concourse,
a mecca for middle-class Gentiles and Jews. It was the
Bronx's only significant boulevard, with a diorama of
Art Deco buildings named after the daughters, wives,
and nieces of their builders—the Beverly, the Diana,
the Rosalind, the Sylvia, the Sandra, the Suzanne—
that sounded to me, in the winter of 1943, like sexy
maidens who might leap from their lettering on a
stone façade and frolic with a boy of five. But to live
off the Concourse, no matter how near, was already
one degree of separation, a mark of decay among the
middle class. I didn't mind that much. I had my own
cosmology. I could navigate like a shooting star and
land in the Beverly's lap.

What did I know? We moved from the Concourse
a year and a half later, into the lower depths of the East

Bronx, and I had the withdrawal symptoms of a junkie. I shivered; the teeth banged inside my head. I missed the maidens, of course, but what bothered me most was the absence of vocabulary. I was stuck in a forlorn land that didn't seem to have much language. No one talked of model airplanes or banana splits or of the next double bill at the Luxor and the Loew's Paradise, or had ever heard of *Going My Way,* the hottest film of '44, starring Bing Crosby as a priest with big ears.

My brother Harve, who was three years older, would stop the prettiest girls on the Grand Concourse and repeat, "Going my way?" They'd smile, because they were familiar with Bing and belonged to the bourgeoisie. Harve, who had high cheekbones, was hard to resist. But nothing like that exchange could have happened in the East Bronx, where my brother was reduced to banditry. He would waylay boys in the street, older boys, bigger boys, and claim whatever was in their pockets— a dime or a piece of string. But he wouldn't seize anything valuable, like a baseball glove. He had a shrewd sense of property, lived within the letter of the law.

I lived like a little prince insofar as my brother's reputation preceded me from school to school. I still didn't have much of a vocabulary. But finally in adulthood, I found my calling: to live inside a house of words—words that were at such a remove from me in the East Bronx that I had to steal from other writers, cannibalizing their houses. And then, in 1992, my mother died, and I had the urge to write about her in her days of glory, when shopkeepers swore it was Joan Crawford walking the streets of the West Bronx in a silver fox coat, and gave her free tickets to the Loew's Paradise. She was indifferent to all that and obsessed with her brother Mordecai, a teacher in Belorusse, who had sent her off to America with the promise that he would join her. He never did. She was constantly looking for letters from him, but the war had killed their correspondence. In midwinter, she would march to the post office in a trance, like an illuminated ghost, wrapped in dark fur with silver spots, and half the West Bronx seemed to swoon in her wake.

I was her guardian, of course. I steered her to the P.O. And what a vocabulary I picked up on those walks, as I stared at posters advertising *Wilson*— a movie about that forlorn president who suffered a stroke and hid in the White House, a much less illuminated ghost than Mom, while his young wife, the second Mrs. Wilson, really ruled the country. EXTRAVAGANZA—CAST OF THOUSANDS—EPIC OF THE YEAR—MRS. WILSON AS AMERICA'S FIRST REGENT—I pulled in those words like a voracious anteater. Words, words, words. It didn't matter what they meant. Each syllable had its own essential music.

With the idea of a memoir about my mother—a book that was published five years ago, as *The Dark Lady of Belorusse*—I revisited the West Bronx; the streets were much wilder than they'd been in 1944. I was no Candide. I'd been back to the Bronx as it burned during the 1970s, when landlords hired thugs to torch their own buildings in order to collect phantom insurance, and then the thugs outdid the landlords and torched buildings to satisfy their own anarchic desires. The place was an endless bonfire. I remember standing on the back porch of my old public school with a panoramic view of the East Bronx and its desert of burnt carcasses, sad versions of the Beverly and the Rosalind.

But in 1992, it was different. The burning had stopped. Buildings rose from the desert, often from their own carcasses. As I stood on my old corner, at Sheridan Avenue and 169th Street, I felt a sudden surge of power, as if I'd regained the lost currency of the Bronx—its language and rituals. That corner seemed minuscule, the territory of a little boy, but it was on a plateau, with hills on three sides, the steepest one climbing toward 168th Street, which was so high that it created its own horizon; for a five-year-old, it would have been like the very edge of the known world. Scaling that hill was the adventure of a lifetime, going from Sheridan to some freshly minted Shanghai, all in five or ten minutes, in that winter of '44, when half the kindergartens were closed because there was a shortage of teachers and I had to read *Bambi* at home in a broken-backed edition with a green cover (I still have it). My vocabulary was the vocabulary of that book, filled with forest words; and the Bronx, with snow on the ground, was a forest floor, with the occasional intrusion of adults and trolley cars. Even within the trolley wire I saw electrical trees, with branches that spat out sparks, and I loved to follow the tracks of a trolley, its traces in the snow. But those adventures never produced any Shanghais.

Why was I entranced with Shanghai? *Bambi* was a cityless book. But China was very much in the news— that is, the news according to *The March of Time,* a regular movie magazine that played at the Loew's Paradise and substituted for kindergarten. As far as I could tell, Shanghai had fallen to the Japanese in 1937, but a guerrilla band that was loyal to no one but itself had built a new Shanghai in the north, with a little boulevard called Bubbling Well Road. The newsreel showed the guerrilla chief, his body laced with ban-doliers, his cheeks scarred and scratched, standing on a street corner not unlike my own, declaring that old Shanghai had lost its right to exist, that it was a male-diction, and from now on his Shanghai would work its way into the nation's memory. To me, it seemed bold to declare a city defunct and simply move it to another corner, with brick and mud and force of mind.

I wanted to be like that scarred man—a Bronx guerrilla who could destroy and rebuild with a bando-lier of words. And I realize now that writing novels is like moving cities, like reinventing Shanghai. What-ever feel I have for adventure I owe to the odd tilt of a street corner, like some genetic code of imagination, luring me to master the unknown.

For a confused boy who had just discovered words, *Bambi* was more disturbing and real than any kindergarten. I wanted to hunt the hunters who'd destroyed Bambi's mom, but I wanted to do it with my ammunition—words I could pluck from a movie poster, or take from the mouth of the manager at the P.O., who would take me on trips to the "graveyard," a gigantic sack filled with undeliverable letters I longed to read.

Harve had all the privileges a reader would want. He was in the third grade, which hadn't been cancelled. But he'd passed beyond that period of verbal enchantment. He was almost an adult, a sea scout considering a career in the navy, a troubadour who could trouble pretty girls, while I was completely idle, without school, without ambition, an anteater sucking in words like crazy, as Woodrow Wilson sat beleaguered in the White House—screen time had its own sense of eternity—and I wandered my corner, below the Concourse, looking for Shanghai.

Author's note: From "The Writing Life," edited by Marie Arana, *The Washington Post*, 2003.

Letter from Mogilev
(1997)

W E WOULD WALK THE STREETS, a prodigy in short pants and his mother, so defiantly beautiful that all transactions stopped, and we'd enter a slow-motion world where women, men, children, dogs, cats, and firemen in their trucks would look at her with such longing in their eyes that I felt like some usurper who was carrying her off to another hill. I was only five in '42, a nervous boy who couldn't spell his own name. My mother wore her silver fox coat, designed and cut for her by my father, Sam, who was a foreman in a Manhattan fur shop. The coat was contraband, and should have gone to the navy. My father's shop had a contract with the War Department to supply the navy with fur-lined vests so its admirals and ordinary sailors wouldn't freeze to death aboard some battleship.

It was a darkly romantic time. The Bronx sat near the Atlantic Ocean, without a proper seawall, and there was talk of attack squads arriving in little rubber boats off some tricky submarine, getting into the sewer system, and gobbling up my native ground. But I never saw a Nazi on our walks. And what power would any of them have had against the shimmering outline of my mother in her silver fox coat? She was born in 1911, like Ginger Rogers and Jean Harlow, but she didn't have their platinum look; she was the dark lady from Belorusse.

We weren't on a pleasure stroll. It was our daily trip to the post office, where my mother was expecting a letter from Mogilev, in White Russia, where her brother lived, a schoolteacher who'd raised her after their own mother had died. I'm not sure why this letter couldn't have been delivered to the mailbox in our building. Had the Germans seized Mogilev, and my uncle could only write via some secret system in the Soviet underground?

The postmaster would always come out from behind his window when my mother appeared. He was a cranky little man who wore slippers and liked to shout at his clerks. But he was kind to the dark lady's little boy. He would take me through his side of the wall and show me the "graveyard," a gigantic sack where all the dead letters lay, sad, undeliverable things, with postmarks from all over the planet. I would sift through the pile, look at the pictures on the stamps, and smell the glue while the postmaster squeezed my mother's hand. But not even this wizard of the mail could produce a letter from Mogilev.

She would tremble on the journey home as we climbed hill after hill. She walked like a drunken lady.

It was from my mother that I learned how memory could kill. She could survive as long as she had word from Mogilev. But there was no word in the middle of a war, only mountains of dead-letter boxes between Belorusse and the Bronx.

She started smoking cigarettes. And I had to smother a fallen match and slap at the little fires that seemed to collect in her wake. I would dust the walls with a dry mop and attend to my mother's goose, opening the oven door to stab at the bird with a fork until it was the way my father liked it, dark and crisp and unchewable.

I would put his whiskey on the table, pour him a shot, and jabber endlessly, ask him whatever non-sense came into my head, to camouflage my mother's silences. But as soon as he left the house, she would pretend that her brother was calling from Mogilev (we didn't even have a telephone), and she'd laugh and cry in a Russian that was so melodious, I would get con-fused until I believed that *all* language was born on a phantom phone.

Her English had no music; it was halting and cruel, like a twisted tongue. But I was a clever little bastard. I would clutch at her phrases like building blocks and sing my own backward sentence-songs. "In the sea, Mama, drowns many broken ships." I'd never been to the sea. But I could imagine the great Atlantic, where those German subs prowled like crocodiles. My mother had promised to take me across the bridge into Manhattan and watch the ocean liners that lay hobbled in the Hudson and couldn't get into the war. But there was always that letter from Mogilev on her mind, and she didn't seem able to plot the simple logic of our trip.

And so we were marooned in the Bronx. My mother got more morose. She would stand in front of the mirror for an hour with a pot of rouge and a canister of lipstick and paint her face. Then she'd start to cry and ruin all the work she did, enormous teardrops eating into the paint with their own salty acid. I'd follow her into the street and head for the post office, people staring at this flaw in the dark lady, the tracks in her face. It couldn't have made her less appealing, because the postmaster was twice as attentive.

"Some coffee, Mrs. Charyn?" he said, and coffee was hard to find. He'd have pieces of candy for me, and cups of cocoa, which marked my own lips. But my mother was deeply discouraged. The pain had eaten into her ritual.

"No letter Mogilev?"

"It will come, Mrs. Charyn. Russian letters are notorious. They ride very slow, but they never fail."

He'd dance around her in his slippers, scowl at his clerks, pirouette with his coffeepot, but my mother hardly noticed. She hadn't risked disappointment day after day to become part of his coffee club. He couldn't have charmed her with all the candy in the world.

And I was lost at sea. I had to pilot my mother from place to place, undress her, cook my father's goose. But

I was getting lucky. I didn't have to go to school. Kindergarten had been canceled in the Bronx. There was a terrible shortage of teachers, and someone must have figured that five-year-olds like me could sit at home with wooden blocks and a pound of clay. I didn't have time for clay. I had to groom my mother, coax her into shape, fool my father into believing she was perfectly fine. I fed him scotch and gin. He was walleyed when he left the dinner table. He would ask my mother questions, and I would answer, once, twice, until I got slapped.

"Mind your business, Baby."

"Baby," that's what he would call his own kid to make him suffer. I couldn't read or write, but I could listen to the radio. I heard the battle reports, how the British commandos were making amphibious landings in the middle of the desert, and knocking the hell out of Hitler's Africa Corps. I asked my father to call me "Soldier" or "Little Sergeant," but he never did.

Dad was the sergeant, not me. Cutting fur-lined vests for a lot of admirals had kept him out of the war, but he still had his own uniform: a white helmet that looked like a shallow pot and a white armband with a complicated insignia (a blue circle with a triangle of red and white stripes sitting inside). My father was an air-raid warden with the rank of sergeant. He would patrol the streets after dark with a silver whistle around his neck and make sure that every single window in his assigned radius of blocks had a blackout curtain. If a light blazed from a window, he'd warn you with his whistle and shout, "Lights out, smarty." And if that didn't work, he could call the cops or summon you before the Civilian Defense Board. He was an impeccable warden, my dad, heartless within his own small hegemony, willing to risk the wrath of friends, neighbors, anyone who misbehaved. He'd herd you into a cellar if he ever caught you in the street during an air-raid drill. Some people wouldn't listen to Sergeant Sam, some rebelled, beat him into the ground until other wardens arrived, or a cop rescued him. Even in 1942, his first year as a warden, he had a medal from Mayor La Guardia, chief of Civilian Defense. I caught La Guardia on the radio. "We have our soldiers in Brooklyn and the Bronx, brave men who go forth without a gun, who guard the home front against saboteurs and unpatriotic people. What would I do without my wardens?"

And if Dad came home with a bruised eye and a broken whistle, his armband torn, a big dent in his white hat, it was Baby who had to search for Mercurochrome, while my mother sat forlorn in the living room, dreaming of Russian mail. He was much more solicitous in moments of sorrow, almost endearing with dirt on his face. He'd clutch my hand and look at FDR's picture on the wall while I swabbed his eye with a cotton stick.

"Baby, shouldn't we write to the president?"

"He's busy, Dad; he's drowning in mail. A warden can't complain. How would it look if you snitch? You'll give the Bronx a bad name."

Of course I couldn't speak in full, flowing sentences.

My melody went something like this: "Drownin', Dad, the prez. Eatin' vanilla envelopes. And you better be quiet. The Bronx will kill a tattytale."

Dad got my drift.

"Who's a tattytale?"

But he wouldn't have slapped me with Franklin Delano Roosevelt on the wall. Even in her distraction, my mother blessed FDR whenever she lit a candle. The blood that flowed in him was our blood, too.

Anyway, Dad couldn't have written to Roosevelt. He was as unlettered as I was, as feeble with the pen. He could barely scratch a few words in his Civilian Defense reports. And so he suffered quietly, licked his wounds, and we went to church on the High Holidays, with his face still black-and-blue. I had to dress my mother, make sure her mascara didn't run. We didn't belong to that temple on the Grand Concourse, Adath Israel, with its white stone pillars and big brass door. Adath Israel was where all the millionaire doctors and lawyers went. The services were held in English. The assistant rabbi at Adath Israel was also a painter and a poet. He gave classes at night for kids in the neighborhood. We called him Len. He was in love with the dark lady. That's why he encouraged me, let me into his class. He wanted us to join the temple, but my father wouldn't go near any place that didn't have a cantor. That was the disadvantage of English. A cantor would have had nothing to sing.

We went to the old synagogue at the bottom of

the hill. It was made of crumbling brick; portions of
the steeple would rain down from the roof. There had
been three fires at the synagogue since the war began,
and the "incendiary bomb," as we called it, was always
about to close. But we had Gilbert Rogovin, who'd been
a choirboy here and had studied at the cantors' college
in Cincinnati, Ohio. Our cantor could have made a fortune singing holy songs on Fifth Avenue, but he always
returned to the Bronx. He was a bigwig at the Cincinnati Opera House. He played Spanish barbers and mad
Moroccan kings when he wasn't with us.

He was married to the diva Marilyn Kraus, and he
would always bring her to our crumbling synagogue.
She was a herculean beauty, six feet tall, with the hands
of a football player and a full, floating figure. When
she trod up to the balcony, where all the women sat,
the stairs shivered under her feet. The balcony was
full of opera fans who worshipped Marilyn, called her
"Desdemona," and I wondered if this Desdemona was
another dark lady from Belorusse.

I had the privilege of sitting with my mother and
all the other women, because I was only five. Desdemona hunkered down next to us on our narrow bench,
her enormous hands cradled in her lap, like a despotic
queen of the balcony. She waved to the cantor, who
wore a white robe and was about to wave back when he
discovered the woman near his wife. The breath seemed
to go out of his body. He was just like those firemen
who had seen my mother for the first time. Lost in her

world of letter boxes, she didn't even smile at him. The cantor was all alone; he couldn't pierce the devotion in her dark eyes. He stood among his choirboys, started to sing. But he wasn't like a postmaster dancing in slippers. He was the custodian of songs. He brought my mother out of her dream with his opening syllables. A woman swooned. I had to run and find her smelling salts. . . .

He leaned against the gate with a cigarette in his mouth. A cantor wasn't allowed to smoke on the High Holidays. But Rogovin could do no wrong. Desdemona wasn't with him. She must have gone back to their suite at the Concourse Plaza. My mother and I had ventured out of the synagogue with Sergeant Sam, who'd become a local hero because of his little calvaries as an air-raid warden. He was like a special policeman with a wounded face. The cantor saluted him. "Sergeant, I'd like to borrow your boy."

None of us had ever been that close to the cantor, who had little white hairs in his nose. He wore a strange perfume, smelled like a certain red flower at the Bronx Zoo.

"It's an honor," my father said. "But how can I help you? The boy is five. He doesn't have working papers. He can't spell."

"It's a sad story. My old mother has been pestering me to have a child. I had to invent one."

"You lied to her, Cantor?"

"It's scandalous. But Mom's half blind, lives at a

258   ♔   In the Shadow of King Saul

nursing home in the Bronx. Have to make Mom happy before she dies."

Rogovin sobbed into his handkerchief. I'd never seen a cantor cry. His tears were the size of my mother's crystal earrings. Dad took pity on him.

"Cantor, please . . . we'll lend you the boy." He turned to my mother in bewildered fury. "Do something. We can't let the cantor choke on his tears."

I'm not sure if my mother was dreaming of Mogilev at that moment. But she came out of her trance long enough to slap Rogovin in the face. Dad was even more perplexed. The wives of air-raid wardens weren't supposed to perform criminal acts, and assaulting cantors in a public place was worse than criminal; it was a sin against God, because God favored a cantor above all other beings. God loved a good song.

My mother slapped him again. Rogovin wasn't surprised. I saw him smile under the hand he used to cover his mouth.

My father made a fist. "I'll kill you," he said to the dark lady.

"Sergeant," the cantor said, "you shouldn't provoke Madame. She'll just go on hitting me."

"I don't understand," Dad said.

"It's simple. My missus was in the balcony with Madame. They got to talking about me . . ."

"Balconies. Missus. I don't understand."

I was just as baffled. I hadn't been able to hear Desdemona whisper a word.

"Foolish," my mother said to Dad. "Is no nursing home, is no blind ladies. His mother eats, drinks like a horse."

"I don't understand."

My mother seized Rogovin's thumb and placed it near her breast. "Is clear now? The cantor is lust and lecher."

Rogovin bowed to me, kissed my hand like some kind of Continental, and ran to his hotel.

MY FATHER HAD BEEN SO DILIGENT in producing fur-lined vests, his boss was sending him to Florida for a week. Most wartime vacations had to be canceled because the army and navy were running munitions and men on the railroads. But Dad had a special pass, signed by Secretary of the Navy Frank Knox. I didn't learn about Florida until a little later—Miami Beach was a furrier's paradise, where manufacturers and their prize workers would have a yearly fling with local prostitutes and dark ladies from Havana and New Orleans. And when I grew aware of the word *prostitute*, around the age of six or seven, I understood the arguments my mother had with Sergeant Sam about his sojourns at the Flagler Hotel. She would hurl a shoe at his head, empty the perfume bottles he'd brought back from Florida, set fire to the photographs he'd hidden in some secret pocket of his valise. He'd always return terrifically tanned, looking like Clark Gable with a guilty grin.

But Gable could have been a ghost in 1942. My mother didn't even watch him pack. He left in a hurry, without his air-raid warden's hat, gave me five single-dollar bills to spend in his absence, a small fortune from one of the navy's favorite sons. I was glad to see him go. I wouldn't have to groom my mother, make her presentable to Dad, hide her sorrow from him, cook his goose, load him down with whiskey so he wouldn't discover her long silences.

The day he was gone, her suitor arrived. I don't know what else to call him. He advertised himself as my uncle, but he didn't have our famous cheekbones and Tatar eyes. He couldn't have belonged to that tribe of Mongolian Jews who terrorized the Caucasus until they were conquered by Tamerlane the Great. Chick Eisenstadt was a big ruddy fellow who'd once worked with my mother in a Manhattan dress shop. She'd been a seamstress before she got married. The whole shop had been in love with her, according to Chick, but he was the one who linked his own history with hers long after the dress shop disappeared. He'd floundered until the war. Chick was the only one of my "relatives" who'd ever been to Sing Sing. It was convenient to have a convict in the family. He could tell you stories of the biggest outlaws. And he knew my father's timetable. He would appear whenever Sergeant Sam wasn't around.

He took us for a ride in his Cadillac. Chick wasn't supposed to have a car. Gasoline had been rationed, and there was a ban on nonessential driving. But Chick was a black marketeer who gave generals and war admin-istrators silk stockings for their wives. He had a card that authorized him to chauffeur "essential people," like doctors and tycoons from war plants. Cops would peek into the Cadillac, glance at my mother, smile, call me "Roosevelt's little pioneer."

We crossed into Manhattan with Chick, who took me to the ocean liners that lay tilted in the harbor, like sleeping beauties with smokestacks, and I was seized with an anxiety I'd never had before. An ocean liner was larger than my imagination. It was like the imprint of a world I couldn't fathom from the Bronx. The one bridge I had was Chick.

He never bribed me, never offered expensive gifts that would have made me despise my own dad. But he took us to the only White Russian restaurant on the Grand Concourse, Bitter Eagles, where his cronies would ogle us; he'd sweat in the middle of a meal, sit-ting with his secret family. Sing Sing had ruined his health. He had a chronic cough, and his hands still shook from the beatings his fellow prisoners had deliv-ered to him. Chick was thirty-five, three years older than my mother, but his hair had gone white in Sing Sing, and he looked like a war-torn cavalier.

He stared at my mother, helpless before her plate of pirogi, and said, "Faigele, what's wrong?" My mother's name was Fannie, but her admirers and friends called her "Faigele," which was supposed to mean "little bird" in my Tatar dictionary.

"Mogilev," my mother said. One word. And Chick could intuit the entire tale.

"Your brother, the schoolteacher. His letters are no longer coming. And you're worried to death."

"The Nazis are sitting in Mogilev," I said. "Chickie, I heard it on the radio."

Chick watched my mother's grief. "Radios can lie. It's called propaganda."

"The Germans are paying the radio to tell lies?"

"I didn't say Germans. It could be the White House. And the president doesn't have to pay. Don't you get it? The president talks about a defeat that never took place. Hitler relaxes and starts to get sloppy. And we turn the tables on him."

I wouldn't argue with Chick. A black marketeer ought to know. But I didn't believe that Roosevelt would ever lie about Mogilev.

"Faigele, if there's a letter, I'll find it."

We went to the post office after lunch. The postmaster stood in his slippers, eying my mother and her black marketeer, who eyed him back. "Mister, could one of your own men have been tampering with the mail?"

"Impossible," the postmaster said as Chick stuffed his pockets with silk stockings.

"Come on, I'll help you look for the letter. It has to be here."

They searched the back room, inspected every pouch, but there were no letters from Mogilev. "I'm sorry, Mrs. Charyn," the postmaster said. "Russian mail has been trickling in, but not a scratch from Belorusse."

Faigele took to her bed. "My two bitter eagles," she mumbled, blinking at me and Chick. It was a complete collapse. Chick's own doctor came, examined her, said he couldn't cure heartbreak and withered emotions. He recommended a rest home in the Catskills where he sent all his worst cases.

"Doc," Chick said, "she's not a case. She's a glorious woman, Faigele. She's expecting a letter from Mogilev."

"You're the wizard. You can produce silk stockings. Why not one lousy letter? But what's it all about? Did she leave a boyfriend behind?"

"A brother," Chickie said.

The doctor rolled his eyes. "Isn't it unnatural to miss a brother so much?"

Chick grabbed him by the collar, and I didn't know it then, but it was a very brave act. This doctor was Meyer Lansky's personal physician. He'd poisoned people for the mob. He was the highest-paid internist in the Bronx.

I brought Chick and him a glass of my father's best schnapps. And then Chick explained to him the story of Faigele and Mordecai, who'd come from a family of small landowners in the Tatar town of Grodno, where Meyer Lansky was born. Mordecai was the oldest at ten, with a couple of kid sisters—Anna, five, and Faigele, two—when their mother died (their dad had run to America and made his own life). A ten-year-old boy couldn't hold on to the family fortune. He had to lease himself, become a little slave to protect his sisters. He was sold into the tzar's army at fifteen, escaped, "kidnapped" Anna and Faigele, hid out with them in the marshes, landed in Mogilev in the middle of the Russian Revolution without papers or a crust of bread. The boy was sixteen and he learned to steal. In a time of shadowlands, he became a shadow until he could reinvent himself as a schoolteacher. He had forged documents from a commissar of education who'd been killed. He had pupils in his first classes who were older than himself. He had to bribe an inspector from Minsk: it was like the tzar's government without a tzar, but the Cossacks had been told by some Soviet prince to love all the Tatar Jews. Mordecai saved his money and was able to send Anna out of Belorusse in 1923. But Faigele wouldn't go. He pleaded with her. The inspectors would catch him soon—an illiterate teacher. He couldn't breathe until his little sister was safe.

"But I am safe," she said, "here with you."

He'd start to cry, this gaunt man who was always on the verge of getting TB. She left for America in 1927. He promised to join her in six months but never did.

She became a Manhattan refugee, lived with her father and a stepmother who begrudged every bit of food she swallowed. She went to night school, worked in a dress shop, dreaming of Mordecai. She had to get out of her father's house. Enter Sam, the furrier who never lost a day's work during the Depression.

Faigele married him, but nothing could sustain her—not children, not God, not romance—nothing except those letters that would arrive religiously from Mogilev.

The doctor licked his schnapps. "Chickie, a glorious woman, righto, but where do you fit in? You're not the husband, you're not the brother, you're not the father of this little boy."

"None your stinking business," said Chick, already drunk. "I fill the empty spaces. I'm satisfied."

"If you want to revive her, friend, you'll just have to forge that letter . . . pretend you're with the tzar's police."

"I don't have to pretend. But how will I get Russian stamps?"

The doctor tapped my skull. "Baby, where's your mother's stash of mail?"

I steered them right to the little wooden chest my mother had brought from Belorusse; the letters were inside. Chick was mainly interested in the stamps and the quality of paper and Mordecai's penmanship, but the doctor began to read the letters in whatever Russian he still had at his command (he was born in Kiev).

"The man's a poet, Chick."

He recited from the letters, but Chick cut him off. "Keep it to yourself, Doc."

"Are you insane? Poetry belongs to the world."

"But the letters belong to Faigele."

Every stamp had a different face. I saw the brown eagle of Belorusse; Tatar princes and kings; Stalin, the

266   IN THE SHADOW OF KING SAUL

little father of his people, looking like a walrus. The doctor pulled a pair of scissors out of his medical bag. He wanted to cut off a few of the stamps; Chick told him to put the scissors back. He wouldn't mutilate my mother's property.

"I give up," the doctor said, while Chick and I went down to the stationery store, where I helped him pick out a blue envelope and a pad that could have passed for Russian paper. Then we walked to Bitter Eagles, found a man who was willing to trade Russian stamps in his family album for the promise of butter, eggs, and Colombian coffee.

Chick went to work practicing Mordecai's pen strokes. Time seemed to clot around him and the letter he was going to write. The doctor abandoned wife, children, mistresses, all his other patients, including Meyer Lansky, to mastermind a letter from Mogilev made in the Bronx. I brewed cups of black tea and fed them coffee cake from Bitter Eagles.

It took Chick an hour to do "Dear Faigele" in Mordecai's Russian hand and get the first paragraph going. They had to tiptoe around the war because Chick wouldn't load the letter with lurid details. "I am only starving a little bit," he wrote in schoolteacher Russian, and signed Mordecai's name. He addressed the envelope, I glued on the stamps, and we all fell asleep in the living room on different chairs.

A knocking sound came right through my dreams. I got up, stumbled to the door. The postmaster stood in his slippers with a letter in his hand. He was very excited. "Gentlemen, it arrived, right out of the blue." Chick offered him some of our fabulous coffee cake, speckled with dark chocolate. "Delicious," he said. No one thanked him for the letter, which had come in a crumpled white envelope, all the stamps missing. The postmaster left. Chick tore up *our* letter and we went in to wake up my mother and give her the other letter from Mogilev.

She danced out of bed like a mermaid with a nightgown on (I'd never seen a mermaid, so I had to imagine one). She savored the letter, but she wouldn't read it until she prepared our tea. The doctor was startled by her metamorphosis. Faigele's coloring had come back. She disappeared into the bedroom and closed the door.

"The angels would be envious of such a creature," the doctor said.

We waited like orphans until my mother came out. She wouldn't share Mordecai's language with us. "Is still schoolteacher," she said, summarizing the plot. "But without school. Was bombed."

The doctor returned to his practice. Chickie had to go out of town. My father got back from Miami with his movie-star tan, but Faigele was the one who had all the flush. He put on his air-raid helmet and patrolled the streets. I imagined him in the blackout, looking for renegade cubes of light. Poor Sergeant Sam, who could never really capture the dark lady, or her radiance.

SELECTED BIBLIOGRAPHY

Babel, Isaac. *The Collected Stories.* Translated by Walter Morrison. Cleveland: Meridian Books, 1960.

———. *The Complete Works of Isaac Babel.* Edited by Nathalie Babel. Translated by Peter Constantine. New York: Norton, 2002.

———. *The Lonely Years 1925–1929.* Edited by Nathalie Babel. Translated by Andrew R. MacAndrew and Max Hayward. Boston: David R. Godine, 1995.

———. *1920 Diary.* Edited by Carol J. Avins. Translated by H. T. Willets. New Haven: Yale University Press, 1995.

———. *You Must Know Everything: Stories 1915–1937.* Edited by Nathalie Babel. Translated by Max Hayward. New York: Dell Publishing, 1970.

Babel, Nathalie. "Afterward: A Personal Memoir." In Isaac Babel, *The Complete Works of Isaac Babel.*

Bellow Saul. *The Adventures of Augie March.* New York: Viking, 1953.

Bloom, Harold, ed. *Modern Critical Views: Isaac Babel.* New York: Chelsea House, 1987.

Brashler, William. *Josh Gibson: A Life in the Negro Leagues.* New York: Harper & Row, 1978.

Carden Patricia. *The Art of Isaac Babel.* Ithaca, NY: Cornell University Press, 1972.

Caro, Robert. A. *The Power Broker: Robert Moses and the Fall of New York.* New York: Vintage Books, 1975.

Clarke, Donald Henderson. *In the Reign of Rothstein*. New York: Vanguard Press, 1929.

Ehre, Milton. *Isaac Babel*. Boston: Twayne, 1986.

Ehrenburg, Ilya. *Memoirs: 1921–1941*. Translated by Tatiana Shebunina. Cleveland: World Publishing, 1964.

——. "The Wise Rabbi." In Harold Bloom. ed., *Modern Critical Views*.

Falen, James. E. *Isaac Babel: Russian Masters of the Short Story*. Knoxville: University of Tennessee Press, 1974.

Fiedler, Leslie, "Saul Bellow." *Prairie Schooner 31* (Summer 1957).

Fitzgerald, F. Scott. *The Great Gatsby*. New York: Charles Scribner's Sons, 1925.

Freidin, Gregory. "Fat Tuesday in Odessa: Isaac Babel's 'Di Grasso.'" In Harold Bloom, ed., *Modern Critical Views*.

Glazer, Nathan, and Daniel Patrick Moynihan. *Beyond the Melting Pot*. Cambridge, Mass: MIT Press, 1970.

Gross, Jane, "Success on the Court Brings Anguish for Yannick Noah," *New York Times*, January 9, 1984.

Howe, Irving. *World of Our Fathers*. New York: Touchstone Books, 1976.

Joselit, Jenna Weissman. *Our Gang: Jewish Crime and the New York Jewish Community, 1900–1940*. Bloomington: University of Indiana Press, 1983.

Koch, Edward I. *Mayor*. New York: Simon & Schuster, 1984.

Koolhaas, Rem. *Delirious New York*. New York: Oxford University Press, 1978.

Mandelstam, Nadezhda. *Hope Against Hope: A Memoir*. Translated by Max Hayward: New York: Atheneum, 1970.

Miller, Gabriel. "Samuel Ornitz." In *Dictionary of Literary Biography*. Vol. 28. Detroit: Gale Research Company, 1984.

Munblit, Georgy, "Reminiscences of Babel." In Isaac Babel, *You Must Know Everything*.

Nikulin, Lev. "Years of Our Life: Babel on His Seventieth Birthday." In Isaac Babel, *You Must Know Everything*.

Ornitz, Samuel. *Haunch Paunch and Jowl*. New York: Boni and Liveright, 1923.

Ozick, Cynthia. *Art and Ardor*. New York: Alfred A. Knopf, 1983.

———. Introduction to Isaac Babel, *The Complete Works of Isaac Babel*.

Pirozhkova, A. N. *At His Side: The Last Years of Isaac Babel*. Translated by Anne Friedman and Robert L. Busch. South Royalton, VT: Steerforth Press, 1996.

Radzinsky, Edvard. *Stalin*. Translated by H. T. Willets. Reprint. London: Septre, 1997.

Roth, Henry. *Call It Sleep*. New York: Avon, 1964.

Shentalinsky, Vitaly. *Arrested Voices: Resurrecting the Disappeared Writers of the Soviet Union*. Translated by John Crowfoot. New York: The Free Press, 1993.

Tifft, Wilton and Thomas Dunne. *Ellis Island*. New York: Norton, 1971.

Trilling, Lionel. Introduction to Isaac Babel, *The Collected Stories of Isaac Babel*.

Warshow, Robert. *The Immediate Experience*. Garden City, NY: Doubleday, 1962.

Wolfe, Kevin. "Island of Dreams," *Metropolis*, January–February 2005.

Yezierska, Anzia. *Hungry Hearts*. London: Forgotten Books, 2017.

———. *Red Ribbon on a White Horse*. New York: Persea, 2004.

Zion, Sidney. Interview with the author, July 20, 1985.

BELLEVUE LITERARY PRESS is devoted to publishing
literary fiction and nonfiction at the intersection of
the arts and sciences because we believe that science and
the humanities are natural companions for understanding
the human experience. With each book we publish, our
goal is to foster a rich, interdisciplinary dialogue that will
forge new tools for thinking and engaging with the world.

To support our press and its mission, and for our full
catalogue of published titles, please visit us at blpress.org.

BELLEVUE LITERARY PRESS
New York